CAST OFF

R. Forsyth and Anthony G. Spencer

authorHOUSE®

AuthorHouse™ UK Ltd.
500 Avebury Boulevard
Central Milton Keynes, MK9 2BE
www.authorhouse.co.uk
Phone: 08001974150

First published by AuthorHouse 8/17/2009

ISBN: 978-1-4389-5661-9 (sc)

Printed in the United States of America
Bloomington, Indiana

This book is printed on acid-free paper.

Contents

PREFACE

When I asked Tony why he had been placed in an Orphanage as a boy, his reply,

"Because nobody wanted me!" moved me so much that from then on I wanted to know why. That was the beginning of my four year commitment to finding out from Tony, his family and his friends, who had actually fathered that unwanted kid and who had not mothered him, but given him away – to strangers.

I have in the process of writing this story of hope and despair come to know the man that boy became and as a result I am convinced that what he had to endure and how he was able to overcome the many obstacles in his lifelong quest to find the father he never knew, is meant to be shared. This memoir about a lively, freckle-faced redheaded troubled boy is actually more than just another story about one of life's little losers. No, it didn't end by him taking the drug, booze and womanizing route and that's why I was in the front line of those pitching to write it.

My thanks to Nita Spencer, Tony's wife. She has played such a vital part in Tony's life and still does. My thanks to Adrian Day, one of their many friends who patiently read and corrected my manuscript and gave valuable suggestions and what would I have done without the time, tremendous effort and expertise that Mark Starnes, aided by Peter Beharrell willingly employed in preparing the manuscript for publication! Thank you Mark and Peter.

I consulted Godfrey Spencer, Tony's older brother, who was also an inmate at the Orphanage. He always looked out for his younger brother while they were together in Fegan's. He was very supportive of what I was trying to do and shared his own still vivid memories of events that affected then both. Sadly, during the writing of the book, he became ill and passed away, but I am so thankful for the contacts I had with him and his encouragement.

My thanks to Peter Barton, Nita's elder brother who was there for me when I asked him to give me his account of the first meeting he had with his future brother-in-law in Cyprus. At the time he was having a well-deserved break from his regiment stationed in Egypt during the Suez Crisis.

Nita's family, the Bartons received Tony with open arms when she invited her young boy friend to her home in Gloucester, especially Dolly – her dear mother, who always had a soft spot for the young lad who had never known a mother's love. He had the joy of being able to call Nita's parents, 'Mum and Dad' and that meant so much to him.

During the course of writing this book it was necessary to contact friends of Tony in Canada for their account of the young Spencer lad who entered their lives during a difficult time of his life. Thank you Donald Johns and Pat Guenther for sharing with me your memories. Tony, his brother and his Aunt stayed for a short time in a convent in Toronto and to my surprise when I contacted the Sisters of St.John the Divine one of them, Sister Nora though now of great age, still remembered the little redheaded evacuee from the U.K. Thank you Sisters for all the kindnesses you showed not only to Tony, but also to the many other Strangers who were able to find refuge in Canada during the Second World War. You are remembered with affection by those you helped and befriended.

I must thank Fegan's for all the Organization has been able to do in the past to help needy boys and families and for continuing to take an interest in them long after they cease to need your help.

My heart goes out to all the Old Fegan Boys who have been good enough to contact me with their own memories of being a Fegan Boy during the time that Tony was there. Some I have had the privilege of meeting. These Fegan Old Boys are now spread out over the globe, but they still come together from time to time for a reunion and they don't forget the old days and one another.

What follows is a memoir – a period of twenty years from 1940 –

1960 in the life of its hero, Anthony Gerald Spencer. I hope you get to know him when you meet him in this his very own story and if you happen to have passed this way yourself, then you will understand and take heart in a fellow traveller's ultimate triumph over tragedy.

R. Forsyth
Jan. 2008

CHAPTER 1

London, 1940

When the war started in September 1939 everybody had expected the worst right away. The black-out curtains were put up every night. No-one went anywhere without their government issue gas mask. Then came 'Operation Pied Piper' and thousands of schoolchildren and mothers with young babies and toddlers were evacuated to safe country places. But nothing happened. Everything went on as before. So the evacuees left the quiet country villages and returned home. That was the 'phoney' war.

But in 1940 the real war was about to begin. Food rationing was introduced in January with sugar, bacon and butter, followed by meat in March. In May of 1940, the failure of British operations in Norway led to a critical Commons debate in which the Government's majority was so reduced that Chamberlain felt obliged to resign. He was replaced by Winston Churchill.

On May 13th people huddled together in family groups around their wireless sets, grit their teeth and gave the small brown box their solemn and undivided attention. As they listened to their Prime Minister, sisters Gladys and Sylvia Butler were both very conscious of the weight of their responsibility for the two small boys playing happily with their toy cars on the mat in the front room.

Gladys tried to get a better reception. The broadcast was being spoiled by a constant crackling noise coming over the airwaves. She was anxious not to miss a word of Mr Churchill's speech.

'We are in the preliminary stage of one of the greatest battles of history,' he said. 'We have to be prepared. In this crisis I would say

to the Nation as I said to those who have joined the Government, I have nothing to offer but Blood, Toil, Tears and Sweat.

We have before us an ordeal of the most grievous kind. Many, many long months of struggle and of suffering. You ask, what is our policy? I will say - it is to wage war, by Sea, by Land and Air, with all our might and with all the strength that God can give us. To wage war against a monstrous tyranny, never surpassed in the dark, lamentable catalogue of human crime. This is our policy. You ask, what is our aim? VICTORY. Victory at all costs, Victory in spite of terror, Victory, however long and hard the road may be, for without victory, there is no survival.'

This momentous speech was followed by a rendering of the National Anthem played by bandsmen of the Coldstream Guards. Men and women, boys and girls who had been listening all over the country, stood up straight and silent. This was their personal response to the crisis that threatened not only their country, but their whole British way of life.

Gladys turned off the wireless. 'What are we going to do about the boys, Sylvia?' she said.

Sylvia frowned. 'Well you know Freda wants them to go to Canada. I can't take them. I have to stay. I'll be needed here as a midwife.'

Gladys sat quietly for a while. She was a spinster like her sister and had always looked after other people's children. As a nanny to the well-to-do her charges were babies and toddlers, but her nephews were lively boys of six and eight. She was particularly concerned about young Anthony. Freda had never taken to her younger son. This was probably due to the fact that her husband had walked out on her just before he was born. He was mischievous, boisterous, a handful. Godfrey seemed older than his eight years. He had an old head on young shoulders. The two brothers were as different as chalk from cheese. But at this time of war they were both needy little boys. They needed her now.

'Anthony, Godfrey, come here, I've got something to tell you,' she called out to her nephews. The boys came running. They were growing lads. Perhaps it was supper time. They were always hungry.

'You know boys, don't you, that there is a war on! Stop fidgeting Anthony and pay attention!' She sighed. 'Auntie Sylvia and I have just been listening to the Prime Minister, Mr Churchill on the wireless - this is no laughing matter Godfrey!'

'I wasn't laughing,' said Godfrey. 'It's Anthony. He keeps on pulling stupid faces and putting his tongue out behind your back Aunt Gladys!'

Gladys looked cross, just for a minute. She so wanted to get over to the boys the seriousness of the situation.

'It is going to be difficult for boys and girls and mums and dads to be safe here. So your Mother and Aunt Sylvia and I think it would be best if you, Anthony, Godfrey and I went to Canada to live while the war is on.'

She paused and looked at the fresh young faces waiting for the enormity of what she had just proposed to sink in.

'Canada,' said Anthony. 'Isn't that a long way away? Will Mummy be coming with us?'

'No, Anthony. Your mother has important work to do and will have to stay here. But it's a beautiful big country with mountains and rivers and very kind people. They have red Indians and their policemen are called 'Mounties' because they all have horses.

'Like cowboys, aunt?' enquired a hopeful Godfrey.'

'I suppose so,' she said. 'We'll have to go on a big ship across the Atlantic ocean. Won't it be exciting boys!'

The six year old red-headed boy was ready to go right away, but Godfrey wasn't quite so sure.

'We'll have to start getting things ready. I'm not exactly sure when we'll be going,' she said, 'but it will be soon, very soon.'

Aunt Gladys found picture books of Canada from the local library to show the boys and together they poured over maps and learned how this far away country became a part of the British Empire. It was preparation for what lay ahead. In the meantime, life had to go on. They would have to wait their turn.

At last the day arrived. They were up early.

Everything was packed. But Gladys knew that the train they had to catch would not be leaving Euston Station until well after dark. The sisters read to the boys, played games with them, took them out for a walk around the block; pulled them apart when they squabbled and fought, but were mightily relieved when it was time to put the black-out curtains in place. An air-raid warden shouted outside his familiar cry, 'Put that light out missus. Don't you know there's a war on!' At last it was time to say their final 'goodbyes'.

'Godfrey, for goodness sake stop being a nuisance. Leave Anthony alone,' said Gladys. It had been a long day. 'Anthony, come here. You look a mess. Pull your socks up. Put your cap on. We're going now.'

Sylvia helped get the luggage outside the front door. She took the last opportunity of telling the boys, to 'be good and do what your aunt Gladys tells you,' knowing full well that her words were falling on deaf ears. Then the taxi arrived, they tumbled into it and were gone. 'Euston station please driver,' said Gladys Butler.

A high-pitched whining noise suddenly broke the spell of euphoria that had enveloped the small group. It grew louder and more shrill until it was an all pervasive ear-splitting wailing. It was an air-raid warning of approaching enemy aircraft. The boys crouched down and put their hands over their ears.

'Shall I take you and the boys to a shelter, Miss?' enquired the friendly driver.

'No,' said Gladys Butler shortly. 'We've got a train to catch!'

The driver made a dash for it through the London streets. Anthony and Godfrey Spencer were scared out of their wits by the sound of the anti-aircraft guns banging away at enemy planes overhead, but somehow Aunt Gladys made them feel safe. She knew what to do, where to go. She'd sort everything out.

Godfrey Spencer, the older of the two Spencer brothers remembers how strange the trains looked standing in Euston Station with sticky tape criss-crossing all the carriage windows like preparation for a big game of noughts and crosses. Everywhere was incredibly dark. London was blacked out. There were crowds and crowds of people. Women with noisy children, soldiers, sailors and airmen. All waiting to get on the train. Godfrey wondered how so many could be packed in, but they were.

All the carriages were dark and dingy and were only lit by a dim blue light bulb by which some of the soldiers were trying to read a newspaper. It was a bit of a squash with children expected to sit on grown-ups laps. Godfrey felt very indignant when a soldier offered him his lap to sit on. He shook his head and went out and stood with the men in uniform filling the corridor - quite unnoticed, as they smoked and laughed and chatted just as if these were normal times.

Aunt Gladys did offer her lap for Anthony to sit on, but he couldn't sit still for a minute. The other occupants in the carriage tried to be friendly to the little chap, but he was restless and couldn't settle. In the end they helped him climb up onto one of the luggage racks where he eventually fell fast asleep. It was a long slow journey to Liverpool.

There was a great hustle and bustle when they finally arrived at Liverpool Docks. A big ship was waiting for them. Gladys hurried the boys up the gangplank without so much as a backward glance. This was to be a new start for the boys away from the harsh realities of war. She had always had 'itchy' feet and thrived on change and challenge. She felt a bit like a kid herself, thrilled with the prospect of going to Canada and wondered, like the boys, what adventures awaited them there.

London 1940 Anthony & Godfrey Spencer

CHAPTER 2

The Journey Across The Atlantic

There were thirty-four war guests on board in their party, fifteen of these being children. The Spencer boys' mother was a personal assistant to an American executive in the British affiliate of the International Business Machines Company. When the war began in earnest in the UK IBM arranged with the Canadian Government for some of their employees' dependants to become war guests for the duration of the war. This is how the boys and their aunt together with others had the opportunity of escaping the dangers to civilians in war-torn England.

It was to prove a hazardous journey. They would be crossing the Atlantic in 1940 when German submarine boats were intent on sinking as many British ships as they could, even if they were on an evacuation mission carrying women and children abroad to safety.

The parents and guardians in their party were calm, but anxious. They knew that their charges would not be safe until they reached the shores of Canada. It was by no means certain that they would make it. But the children remember that journey differently.

Tony Spencer woke early. He tumbled out of his bunk bed eager to leave the confines of the cabin and explore the ship that was taking him, his brother and his aunt all the way across a vast ocean to a new land - Canada. Even the name of the country sounded magical to a little English boy of six. He had been cooped up for days and longed to be free to run about.

Gladys Butler spoke firmly to her nephews:

'Now boys, you are not to run wild. You will stay with our group and there is to be no fighting or I shall bring you both back to the cabin and keep you in. Is that clear? I hope you are listening Anthony!'

'Yes, Aunt Gladys,' they replied dutifully, but as soon as the cabin door was open, Tony was up and away; running up and down the deck, hiding behind the big funnels, climbing ladders and peering into lifeboats - a veritable bundle of restless energy. Godfrey held back. He was a big boy of eight. He didn't want to run about with little six and seven year-olds.

Tony was soon joined by Bruce Lemonde who was travelling to Canada with his sister and mother. They were both of an age, but it was Tony that was noticed. Unfortunately for him, his unruly red hair would always attract unwanted attention and give him away. The youngsters were soon busy playing 'hide and seek'. He was about to climb into a lifeboat when he suddenly found himself being picked up and placed firmly down on his feet in front of a big merchant seaman.

'Gotcha, young man!' he said. 'And what do you think you're doing eh? What's yer name?'

'Anthony Spencer, sir.'

'Well now, Anthony Spencer. I'm going to be keeping a beady eye on you and all the other boys so that you don't go getting into trouble. I'll show yer around, but we all 'ave to keep together, see. I'll tell yer about the *Duchess* - would yer like that?'

'Yes, sir,' said all the boys excitedly.

True to his word, the sailor introduced the *Duchess of Atholl* to a rapt audience.

'She's a fine Canadian Pacific Steamship built in Scotland in 1928,' he said. 'She was launched on November 23rd by the *Duchess of Atholl* herself, after whom' she was named. She made her maiden voyage from Liverpool to Montreal, Canada in July 1930 and 'ere you are all doing the same thing, ten years later. Amazing ain't it!' He looked at the bright eyes and the round young eager faces of his charges wondering as he spoke what the future held for them.

'She was a passenger liner before the war until she was requisitioned in December 1939 for trooping duties. 'Trooping duties' means transporting duties - like taking all of you young 'uns over to Canada. She's one of the famous 'rolling *Duchesses*'. There are four in all. She's fast and she'll need all the speed she can muster to keep the enemy at bay!'

He took them to the side of the ship. They noticed the rolling movement. Tony spied another big ship out in front. There is reason to believe it was the SS *Arandora Star* who had left Liverpool on June 26th in company with the *Duchess of Atholl* also en route to Canada carrying a thousand prisoners of war to Newfoundland.

The irrepressible red-headed six year old shouted and waved. He was thrilled to see the other big ship and the huge waves and to feel the *Duchess* being tossed up and down like the big dipper at a fairground. But it wasn't long before some of the boys began to feel decidedly queasy. Their stomachs heaved as the ship rolled.

'All right lads. Permission to deposit yer breakfast in the briny,' said their minder. 'Lean over the side and do what you have to do!'

Tony's older brother was one of these unfortunates. They were just recovering when there was an almighty 'BOOM!' quickly followed by another - 'BOOM!'

'Lord 'elp us, she's been 'it!' said the seaman. Right in front of their eyes they witnessed the awful effect of war at sea. The SS *Arandora Star* had taken a direct hit by a German torpedo. They saw the wounded ship reel and shudder as if staggering from a mortal blow. Then there was pandemonium! Men and boats were soon being lowered into the seething North Atlantic. Many jumped for their lives. There were more explosions as the boys watched transfixed. Other ships soon arrived at the scene and were engaged in picking up survivors when the gallant *Arandora Star* lurched and went down.

'Right!' said the young sailor, recovering his composure. 'Now we'll make for the upper deck and get on with the serious business of life-jacket drill.'

This had to be instilled into the youngsters so that in the end, they knew what to do without thinking. It could save their lives.

'We had life-jacket drill every day,' Tony recalls, 'but it was only fun to us. Some of the children became seasick, but I soon found my sealegs and led Jack, our minder, a merry dance as I ran here and there exploring. He deserved a medal as he worked his socks off to keep us from falling overboard. I still have the two souvenir sailor dolls he gave my brother and I. I've often wondered since if he was on board when the *Duchess* was torpedoed and sunk in 1942.'

Lifelong friendships were forged on that journey. Gladys Butler got to know Margaret Lemonde and young Bruce Lemonde became Tony's mate. They were two young boys in their element. They loved ships and the sea and in the years to come would be able to make it a way of life, but there was no inkling of it then.

In the days that followed the brave *Duchess* and her crew zig-zagged across the Atlantic and in doing so encountered some rough weather with 40ft waves pounding the decks. At last the day dawned, July 4th 1940 when Tony and Godfrey woke to find that their journey had ended. They had arrived in Canada.

Up on deck the boys were thrilled as the *Duchess* came into the St. Lawrence river to Montreal. 'It was so big and beautiful,' said Tony. 'We couldn't see many houses from the deck though.'

'Make sure you've packed everything boys,' said their Aunt. 'Have you got all your bits and pieces together Anthony - we'll be leaving the ship soon?' She looked at him critically. 'Why can't you ever look smart like Godfrey? You're wearing odd socks again! Well, it's too late to change them now!'

As they came down the gangway a brass band was playing a rousing welcome, but Godfrey and Tony knew that they were in Canada for sure when their eyes alighted on a troop of mounted Canadian policemen resplendent in their scarlet tunics. Like many a boy before him and since, Tony vowed he'd be a 'Mountie' when he grew up.

A cameraman from the TORONTO DAILY STAR was there to take their pictures. Tony's remark - 'Gee - I like to see the flag blowing up there,' was duly noted by a reporter looking for good copy and to their surprise and delight both their pictures and Tony's comment were printed in that famous newspaper the very next day.

After disembarking at Montreal, all the passengers were ushered into a big warehouse where officials and volunteer helpers were waiting to process their papers and arrange for them to proceed to their destination. There were about forty children and they all had to sit with folded arms and wait patiently. Aunt Gladys kept a close eye on her young mischievous nephew. She whispered something in his ear and whatever it was it had a salutary effect because thereafter he kept as quiet as a mouse. But he was greatly relieved when at long last their names were called and they found themselves on the way to Toronto by train.

Now all the children could move, run up and down the corridor and let out excited yells at the new sights greeting them around every bend of the track. No-one could keep them quiet. Suddenly some of the older children started to sing the chorus of a popular song;

'She'll be coming round the mountains when she comes. She'll be coming round the mountains when she comes. She'll be coming round the mountains, Coming round the mountains, Coming

round the mountains when she comes!'

And before you knew it, just about everybody in their carriage was joining in. Godfrey and Tony noticed that even Aunt Gladys and Mrs Lemonde were laughing and singing. They reckoned that it was right and proper. After all they had got across the Atlantic ocean safely even though it was swarming with German U-boats and had come to a new land where everything was bigger and brighter than back home. You couldn't help feeling on top of the world! The humming train brought them to a thriving city full of energetic and proud Canadian citizens who still cherished their links with Great Britain and the Empire.

Gladys Butler reckoned it would have done the hearts good of all those left behind back home to have seen the news and pictures on the front page of the TORONTO DAILY STAR:

It's pages were devoted to news of the war in Europe as if it were happening in their own back yard and what is more, there were firm pledges of support for Great Britain in her time of need.

'Well boys, here we are,' said Gladys Butler to her nephews with a twinkle in her eye and a big grin on her face. Pretending to be an important newspaper reporter with notebook and pencil in hand she enquired:

'And what do you young gentlemen think of Canada so far?'

Duchess of Atholl 1940

Evacuees en route to Canada

SAW R.A.F. BOMB U-BOAT NEAR SHIP OF QUEEN'S KIN

Three Days Out When Submarine Sighted, Hamilton Woman Says

687 KIDS ABOARD

Special to The Star

Hamilton, July 6.—The ship which brought the Queen's niece and nephew and 685 other children to Canada was saved by R.A.F. bombs from a German submarine that tried to sink it.

This was revealed here today by Mrs. Joseph Peace, Romford, Essex, and formerly of Hamilton, who crossed on the liner that reached Montreal Wednesday with the first "war guests".

"We were three days out when the submarine was sighted," Mrs. Peace said. "We could see the conning tower. Three British planes from escort vessels immediately began dropping bombs, and the captain said the submarine had been sunk. We didn't see it again."

With Mrs. Peace was her 10-year-old daughter, Margaret, who, though a native of Hamilton, has been in England since she was three. Her father is joining the British army next month.

The ship they crossed on had among its 685 child passengers Davina Bowes-Lyon, 10, and Simon Bowes-Lyon, 8, children of the Queen's brother, David. They were accompanied by their grandmother, Mrs. Spender-Clay and were on their way to New York where they will be guests of J. P. Morgan. The vessel also carried many titled folk.

Voyage to Canada

18

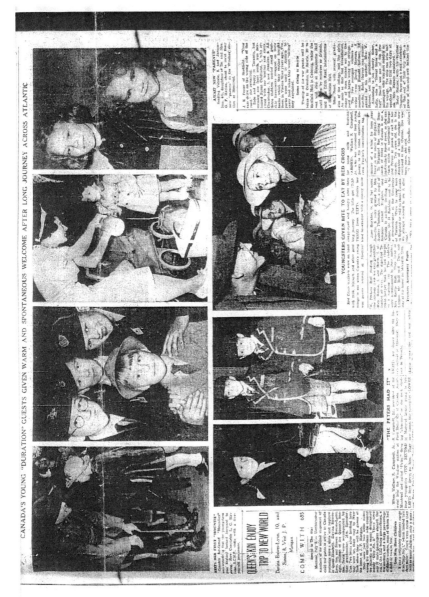

Arrival in Canada

CHAPTER 3

Toronto - Canada

On arrival in Toronto, some of the war guests went straight to their new homes. Others went to stay temporarily at the Convent of St. John the Divine until accommodation within their budget could be found. Gladys Butler and her two nephews were among these.

'Welcome to Canada. We hope you'll be very happy here,' said Sister Maribel and her bright eyes and happy smile accompanied the greeting. 'Did you have a good trip across the Atlantic? Was the weather rough? Do you have any folks in Canada?' Her enthusiasm related to the fact that she originally hailed from England.

'Sister Maribel, leave them alone for goodness sake,' said Sister Nora. 'They haven't been in the country for more than five minutes!'

There was a lot going on. Streams of war guests were arriving and were wondering where they should go and what they should do. They were bewildered to say the least. Margaret Lemonde and her two children spotted Gladys Butler and her nephews. That made her feel better.

'Gladys, Gladys Butler,' she called out.

Gladys Butler turned around and was relieved to find a familiar face in the crowd. She smiled and waved.

'Come, I'll show you to your rooms,' said Sister Joanna, a bright shiny-faced bespectacled nun.

The Spencer boys and their aunt were allocated a two-bedroomed apartment with their own bathroom. It even had a little balcony. Gladys looked around. Her room contained a bed, a small bedside table and lamp; an old chest of drawers, a built-in wardrobe and an old rickety chair. The wooden floor boards were covered with colourful homespun rag rugs. She sighed. Who would have thought that she of all people would have wound up in a convent. Not her scene at all. She didn't have any time for 'church' and all that sort of thing, but if pushed she would have said that she believed in something. She just wasn't sure what that 'Something' was.

'Why are we having to stay in this place?' moaned Anthony. 'I don't like being in a convent. It's full of funny old ladies called nuns.'

'Oh it won't be for long,' said his aunt. 'There's a lot of us coming into the country and it'll take a bit of time for us all to find work and a place to live. In the meantime, you boys make yourselves useful. Unpack your bags. Change your clothes and then we can all go downstairs.

The boys were soon jumping and bouncing up and down on their beds and throwing pillows at each other. Then Godfrey pulled off one of his shoes and hurled it at his brother's head. He scored a direct hit. 'POW WOW!' he cried, 'BULL's EYE!'

Anthony didn't have red hair for nothing. Once provoked, riled, he would catapult into action. He threw himself onto his brother and began pummelling him with all his might, fully expecting him to cry out for mercy.

'You couldn't hurt a flea, you couldn't hurt a flea!' shouted his brother whereupon, Anthony bashed him some more, but he was only six and not yet ready to fight big battles. They would have to come later.

'Oh stop it, the pair of you, said their Aunt. 'I'm going downstairs. They're laying on a feast for us and I'm dying for a cup of tea!'

That was enough to pull them up short. FOOD glorious FOOD!

They slid down the banisters and were away before Gladys could say another word, chasing each other through the convent garden, opening doors - some marked 'PRIVATE'; running down cloistered corridors and bumping into a cluster of nuns. 'Sorry!' they managed before bounding on. They only slowed down when they saw crowds moving towards a big marquee. They guessed rightly. This was the Big Food Tent. Inside they found long trestle tables heavily laden with cooked hams, roasted chickens, colourful salads; heaps of bread and butter and bowls and bowls of fresh fruit, including bananas! There were also new treats awaiting the war guests such as peanut butter. They piled their plates high as if they were afraid that all this largesse might suddenly disappear and be replaced with Spam and hard rock cakes. 'What have you got there?' Anthony enquired of his pal, Bruce Lemonde. 'Ice cream and maple syrup!' He replied. 'It's absolutely scrumptious!'

In that summer of 1940 the sisters were not only offering temporary hospitality to war guests, but were also caring for some children who had learning difficulties. They were a mixed bunch of boys and girls of different ages, but they all felt at home and safe in the convent. The new influx of people known as 'war guests' made them feel very nervous and frightened. It was part of the sisters' task to help all the children get on well together while they had to make the convent their home. Sister Maribel, a young nun, full of life and boundless energy, knew just the thing to make all of her young charges feel right at home. 'We're going to play a game,' she announced. A troop of eager children followed her into the big hall to find balls and bats and funny things that she called, 'stumps' and 'bails'.

After a bit of instruction in the rules of the game - 'cricket' - not well known to most of her charges, the children were soon all laughing and yelling and running about. The bigger boys were allowed to bat first and get the runs while the little 'uns were encouraged and helped by the sisters to bowl and catch them out. Godfrey Spencer was more than a little surprised to find that Sister Maribel and Sister Joanna could hit the ball and run as well as any of the boys. But he was furious when one of the older sisters caught him out.

Later that night after a hot bath, the boys tumbled into bed exhausted. 'I'll never be able to sleep in this bed,' moaned Anthony.

'The mattress is as hard as a board!' But his brother didn't reply. He had gone out like a light as soon as his head hit the pillow.

'Go to sleep Anthony!' yelled his Aunt exasperated. 'I can't Aunt Gladys,' he yelled back. 'Well then, stay awake, but be quiet about it!' she insisted.

When she was sure that both her charges were 'dead to the world', she got her handbag and went downstairs to find Margaret Lemonde and anybody else for a chat.

A crowd of women were sitting on comfortable chairs in a big hall that had been made into a lounge with tables laden with local papers and leaflets full of useful information for the new guests.

Some of the sisters came in and joined them. Gladys Butler was the first to raise the question that was uppermost in the minds of all the new arrivals. 'Can you please tell us how long we have to stay here? she asked.

Sister Hannah smiled at the ladies. 'In the coming days,' she said, 'we'll be organising some trips out in Toronto for you all to have a look around. We'll be showing you where the civic offices are; the schools, the hospitals and of course the shops. We'll take you to our public library and generally help you to find out about our Canadian way of life before we encourage you to leave us and make your own way. This should take about a month or so.'

'A month, a whole month!' cried Jessie Cook in disbelief. The women looked at one another aghast. They had hoped to be able to move out and into their own place within a week!

'Yes, it must seem a long time to you,' continued Sister Hannah, but with so many war guests arriving each day, it will take time to help all of you find work and suitable accommodation.

'We sisters would welcome any volunteers among you who could help us in the kitchen with the cooking or cleaning or in helping to run programmes to keep the children happily occupied. I'll leave you now and hope you sleep well.'

Sister Hannah left the hall, but quickly returned as if she had

23

just remembered something very important that she had forgotten to mention. 'There is just one more thing,' she said.

'Please do not smoke inside any of our buildings, but you may smoke outside in the gardens. Goodnight!'

'Well, did you hear that!' said Jessie Cook who enjoyed a cigarette with her cup of tea and had no intention of going outside in any convent garden to have a smoke. 'I sincerely hope we don't have to stay cooped up here with a whole bunch of nuns for ever. It would drive me bonkers!'

'I suppose we do need to know more about how they do things out here in Canada and where we can best fit into the scheme of things,' said Margaret Lemonde diplomatically.

'Well, I think I'll be turning in,' said Gladys to Margaret, 'see you in the morning.'

As she lay on the hair-mattress on her narrow iron bedstead, Gladys Butler had a few qualms. Had she done the right thing in coming to Canada? How would it all pan out? Would she be able to find work? It seemed to take her ages to get off to sleep and when she did she was back on board the rolling Duchess caught in a terrible storm and feeling as sick as a dog.

'Wake up Aunt Gladys! Wake up!' said Anthony. 'We're starving. We've been ready for ages and want to go down for breakfast!'

When they entered the Dining Room, it was clear from the lively chatter and laughter that everybody felt better. They had a noisy breakfast with children jumping up and down and running in and out. Most of the women were only too pleased to sign up for volunteer work. Gladys Butler opted to help in the kitchen and was pleased to find herself working alongside the young and chirpy sister, Maribelle.

While they were busy peeling a mountain of potatoes, Sister Maribelle thought it would be a good opportunity of getting to know her helper.

'You're the Spencer boys aunt aren't you?' she enquired.

'Yes,' said Gladys. 'They're my Sister Freda's boys. She has an important job and couldn't bring them so she asked me. I trained as a nurse, but I've spent most of my working life as a nanny looking after other people's children.'

'You never married then?' asked Sister Maribelle.

Gladys thought this question was a bit cheeky coming from a nun, but she took it on the chin. 'No,' she said, 'my fiancé was killed just before the end of the First World War, so I never married.' 'I am sorry,' said the young sister, going a bit red. She hadn't meant to embarrass Miss Butler.

'Tell me about your nephews,' the sister asked.

'The youngest, Anthony he's six and a half and quite a handful,' said Gladys. 'He's never still, always up to mischief. He's a red-headed little monster. Godfrey is a few years older and nothing like his brother. He's bookish and very bright. He's going to do well!'

'I'm sure with your support and encouragement, Anthony will do well too, Miss Butler,' said Sister Maribelle with a twinkle in her grey eyes, 'even though at the moment he's fully occupied being a little monster!'

Gladys shrugged her shoulders and grinned. Sister Maribelle was obviously not your run-of-the-mill kind of nun. She was of the boisterous mischievous variety and Gladys reckoned that they were probably thin on the ground in most convents.

After they had filled six large saucepans with peeled potatoes, Gladys was beginning to flag a little when she was saved by the bell. Everybody in the convent kitchen downed tools and Gladys was very happy to discover that even in Canada, everything stopped for the mid-morning coffee break. 'You're quite civilised out here after all,' she said. 'I was beginning to have my doubts!' The following days and weeks sped by. Gladys was willing to turn her hand to anything. She was offered hospital work or training to become a telephonist. She surprised herself by opting for the latter. She had the sneaky idea that it would be more fun because it was different to anything she'd ever done before and so it proved.

One day when she arrived back at the convent, she found Anthony and Godfrey at each others throats, again. 'What's going on here?' she enquired crossly.

'I just called Anthony a sissy and he is,' said Godfrey with a big silly grin all over his face. 'He's been snivelling again because his best friend Brucie has left the convent.'

Anthony lunged at his brother, Godfrey moved smartly out of the way and he landed with a bump on the floor.

Then he began to shout and cry with rage.

'I hate this place. I want to go back home. This isn't Canada!'

'Calm down, Anthony,' said his Aunt. 'I've got some good news for the pair of you.'

Anthony stared straight ahead and folded his arms across his chest. He didn't care. He hated everything and everyone, especially his rotten brother.

Godfrey on the other hand was mildly curious.

'I went to look at a flat today and I've paid the first month's rent in advance. It's ours. Look, I've got the keys!' and she dangled them in front of their noses.

'Really, really and truly?' said Anthony wistfully. He was beginning to think that they would be stuck in the convent for ever and ever.

'You've done it Aunt Gladys. You're amazing!' said Godfrey, grinning from ear to ear.

The next morning, the boys were up, washed, dressed packed and ready to go hours before breakfast. They were sky high with excitement. Now they'd be able to meet Canadian kids and attend regular school and live in the furnished apartment Aunt Gladys had found for them at 1488 King Street, Toronto. What was holding them up? 'Thank you for all you've done for us,' said Gladys Butler to the Sisters with tears in her eyes. 'You've all been absolutely marvellous and I'll never forget you.' 'You'll drop by sometime and let us know how you're making out?' said sister Maribelle.

Aunt Gladys gave sister Maribelle a big hug and then they were both crying.

Anthony Spencer could bear it no longer. 'Oh come on Aunt Gladys,' he said loudly. 'You ladies go on and on. For goodness sake LET's GO!'

St Johns Convent - Toronto

CHAPTER 4

Fun and Games

As soon as the Spencer boys and their Aunt moved into 1488 King Street, Toronto, things began to look up. It was a bright 2-bedroomed apartment on the first floor of a detached property. They made themselves known to their immediate neighbours who were friendly and welcoming. 'If you need anything, you just let us know,' they said. On the ground floor at 1488 was a middle aged couple who had raised three boys, so Gladys reckoned they would be sympathetic towards her boisterous nephews.

'Yes, we come from England,' she said in answer to their enquiries. 'No, the boys are not mine exactly, I'm their aunt!'

The neighbours next door invited them in right away. They were offered drinks and cookies and the young Mum was pleased when Godfrey and Tony played with her twins.

The Spencer boys found that they still had to share bedroom space, but the room was big and airy with a high ceiling and a huge window which looked out onto their busy road. They soon settled in and it wasn't long before they were on their way to school. For starters they found that they didn't have to wear school uniform. That came as a great relief. However, they did stand out from the crowd because of their strong English accent which was impossible to disguise. The Canadian boys had a field day taunting them and trying to mimic them. But they were also a little in awe of the new English kids.

'What was it like crossing the Atlantic?' enquired one of the boys who had yet to venture outside Ontario.

'It was all right,' said Godfrey, 'except that the ship crossing with us was torpedoed and sunk right in front of our eyes!'

'Wow!' said the boys. 'Weren't you kinda scared that you might be next?'

'Not really,' said Anthony who was called, 'Tony' by his new mates. 'We had a lot of fun on board. The sea was very rough, but I never got seasick - Godfrey did though!' He grinned at his brother who scowled back at him.

The Canadian children knew of course that Great Britain and Canada were at war with Germany. Some of their own brothers and uncles had joined-up and were serving overseas, but it didn't really affect the way they lived their lives. Everything went on much the same as usual for the children of Toronto.

Winter came and with it, tons and tons of snow. Tony and Godfrey had seen snow before back in England, but not like this. The lakes and rivers were frozen over. The temperature dropped to well below zero and that's when they realised why the Canadian kids were all togged up in thick warm jackets, high boots and leather hats with ear flaps. At first they had thought this get-up was kind of silly, but they were soon begging their Aunt Gladys for similar outdoor wear! Tony in particular loved the outdoor life in Canada and was soon learning to ice skate, to ski, to play ice hockey and to experience all the thrills and spills of sledging.

Their Aunt was not always able to be around to supervise her nephews after school and at the week-end when she was working. She relied on her good neighbours to keep an eye on them, but this wasn't always easy. They would squabble and fight and at other times would go off with their new friends without informing the neighbours. But the snowballing incident, seemingly innocuous in itself, brought things to a head.

It happened one week-end. Godfrey and Tony were playing further down their road where the local shops were. One of the shops had a big double-fronted window displaying cars for sale. The boys had often pressed their noses against the glass window, dreaming of the day in the distant future when they would be able to have one of their very own.

Godfrey threw a large snowball at his brother which contained a stone the size of a boy's fist. Tony had often been on the receiving end of similar loaded snowballs. He saw it coming and ducked. Crash! Bang! Wallop! It went straight through the big shiny double- fronted shop window like a guided missile.

A very tall, well-built car salesman soon came out into the street to find the little blighters who had done the dastardly deed. 'He saw us sneaking away and shouted after us to stop,' said Tony. 'At first we hesitated, but seeing a big guy whose face was red with rage, we just took to our heels and scarpered!' The big burly Canadian took off after them until he caught up with the bigger boy and collared him.

'What do you think you're doing, kid?' he said angrily. 'I want your name and address. Someone's going to have to pay for what you did today!'

In the meantime, Tony seeing his brother in trouble had returned to the scene of the crime and heard his brother giving his captor a fictitious name and address. He chose this unforgettable moment to go up to the Canadian and volunteer:

'That's not right. He's my brother. We both live at 1488 King Street with our Aunt Gladys. He's Godfrey Spencer and my name is Anthony!'

'Godfrey Spencer couldn't believe his ears. He was absolutely livid with his brother. 'Shut up! You rotten spoil sport!' he shouted at him. 'Now you've got us into real trouble, you stupid squirt!'

'You are so right, wise guy!' said the salesman. He marched them right up the hill to confront their guardian, Gladys Butler.

Gladys Butler who was at home, was duly informed of her nephews' misdemeanour. 'We were only playing snowballs Aunt Gladys. It was an accident!' interjected an unrepentant Godfrey. It was no good her smiling and chuckling and reminding the car salesman that 'boys will be boys'. She tried this tack on the big burly Canadian, but it made no impression upon him whatsoever; if anything it riled him even more. 'Yes,' he said, 'I know about boys. I've got some of my own, but they don't go around breaking shop front windows, running away and then when caught telling blatant lies about who they are and where they live. I can tell you, if my boys did that they'd get a tanning!'

'Really!' said Gladys, 'so much fuss about a broken window.' She turned on her heel and went inside and closed the door, not waiting for any further unpleasantness and to her mind totally unnecessary outburst.

'You haven't heard the last of this,' shouted the big man after her, 'letting those boys run wild in the streets, damaging private property. I'll be billing you for a replacement window and believe me, it's a very big window!' Even behind the door, she heard him. The whole street heard him. He was shouting his head off.

There had been other 'incidents' involving the boys, but this time her nephews had been publicly accused of running wild and damaging private property. Gladys Butler had come to the end of her patience. She would have to find another home for the boys. She couldn't work herself to a frazzle to support them and play nursemaid around the clock too!

'Well,' she said, tight-lipped and as cross as they had ever seen her. 'You've done it now. This is not working. You both need to be in a home and looked after by people who will be very firm with you and stop you making trouble. I'll look into it, first thing in the morning.'

Later that night, Anthony asked his brother - 'What did Aunt Gladys mean? Is she going to put us into a Home for Bad Boys?'

'She's going to put you into a home for boys who tell tales, you stupid kid,' Godfrey answered, 'now shut-up, you get on my nerves!'

*Aunt Gladys - Bruce &
Margaret Lemonde & Boys*

*Aunt Gladys & Boys 1488
Kings Street*

Auntie Gladys on ice

Aunt Gladys Freda Spencer and her boys

Chapter 5

The Lawrences

Tony Spencer woke with a start and looked across at his brother who was still sound asleep. He wondered whether or not to wake him, but thought better of it. Today was going to be scary. Aunt Gladys was taking him and Godfrey to a foster home. She hadn't told them much about it, but he knew he wouldn't be coming back to this place, this room, this street. He sighed, turned over and went back to sleep.

'Happy birthday squirt!' shouted Godfrey and threw a pillow at his brother, swiftly followed by his slippers. It was February 8th, 1941 and Tony's seventh birthday.

'C'mon boys. Get up. We're off today, remember?' said Gladys Butler.

'It's Anthony's birthday today Aunt Gladys,' said Godfrey wondering if she had remembered.

'I know, I know!' she said. 'There's a parcel with your name on it on the kitchen table Anthony. I can't think who it could be from!'

That was more like it. Tony jumped out of bed, rushed through his washing and dressing and bounded into the kitchen. On the table were two parcels, a small one and a biggish one.

He opened the bigger one first. It was a box containing the kit of a model boat with a picture and all the instructions. He read the note inscribed by the sender, Aunt Gladys. 'To Anthony with love.' He ran up and gave her a big kiss. 'Thank you auntie,' he said.

'The other one is from me,' said Godfrey. 'It's a big bar of chocolate. Don't scoff all of it!'

Tony tore open the wrapping and the two of them ate it in double quick time.

'Hurry up and eat your breakfast. The Lawrences are expecting us early,' said Gladys. 'Don't leave anything behind. Remember you'll be staying with these kind people until the war is over!'

'Aren't we ever coming back here to visit?' enquired Godfrey.

'No,' she said. 'It'll be better if I visit you and take you both out now and again. I have to work boys!'

'But supposing they don't like us and want to give us back?' said Tony anxiously, remembering he was apt to get into all sorts of scrapes which invariably made adults very angry with him. 'Well, you'll just have to behave yourselves, won't you!' said Gladys.

'But we might not like them!' said Godfrey sullenly.

'I don't want to go,' said Tony suddenly feeling very miserable and frightened, even on his birthday.

'That's enough of that,' said their aunt. 'It's settled and there's nothing more to be said.'

When they arrived at the Lawrence's bungalow on Latimer Avenue, both of her nephews were reluctant to follow her up the drive to the door.

'They're old and they don't have any kids of their own. It's going to be rotten living here!' said Godfrey churlishly. 'Hello, Miss Butler,' said a plump cheerful looking lady at the door. 'Hello boys, come in. We've been getting so excited waiting for you. We were up with the lark!'

Godfrey went in first with a dark glowering look all over his face, followed by a tight-lipped anxious Tony. 'First let me introduce you to another newcomer to our family. This is Spot. She's just a puppy. I hope you like animals, boys?'

Spot seemed to go straight for Tony. She yapped and jumped up at him, inviting him to stroke her and make a fuss of her. What a birthday surprise! He didn't know the Lawrences' had a puppy. He bent down and took her up into his arms. It was love at first sight and from that time on they were inseparable.

'I'm Lilian and this is Eli, my husand,' said Lilian Lawrence mostly to Godfrey.

'Hello there and what's your name?' enquired Eli Lawrence. 'Godfrey Spencer,' said Godfrey coldly. 'My brother is seven today and he's called Anthony!'

Lilian Lawrence smiled. 'Your Aunt Gladys told us it was Anthony's birthday on the 8th so we've invited a few friends round to meet you. You'll like our neighbours the Johns. They've got a boy called Don, he's seven and a daughter called Pat. She's only a little girl of five, but a real sweetie.'

'I'm much older than them,' said Godfrey emphatically. 'I'm nearly nine and a half.'

The Lawrences looked at each other and grinned. 'Yes, we can see that you're a big boy,' they said.

They had emigrated to Canada way back in the 1920s from Birmingham in the Midlands. Eli was a skilled engineering worker. He soon landed a good job working for De Havillands building aircraft engines. He'd worked hard over the years and was currently a foreman at the plant just outside Toronto.

The couple had expected children to come along, but having reached their late forties still childless had given up hope of ever becoming parents. However, they were happy together and felt they could offer a couple of kids who only had a spinster aunt for company, a secure and loving home.

Gladys stayed a while and saw the boys into their new bedroom which they had to share. Godfrey had been hoping for a bedroom on his own. He felt aggrieved and said so. 'I don't like sharing a bedroom with Anthony. He's a noisy nuisance and he's just a kid.'

Gladys was cross. She took him aside. 'You are being so rude Godfrey, I'm ashamed of you. You say you are a big boy, so act like one! You can be nice and sensible when you want to!'

'I don't want to be nice and sensible,' he retorted and plonked himself down on his bed and turned his face to the wall.'

'I think it'll be better if I just leave them to get to know you without my breathing down their necks,' said Gladys Butler. 'It'll take a little time, but I'm sure they'll be all right.'

At the end of that first day, the Lawrences relaxed a little as they got ready for bed. 'Well,' said Eli, 'it seemed to go all right.' 'Yes, Tony is going to be easy,' said Lilian. 'He just loves Spot and she loves him, but his brother worries me a bit. Something's eating him. He's out of sorts; angry with his aunt, angry with us, angry with his brother!'

''We'll give him a wide berth and leave him to cool off for a few days,' said Eli. 'He'll come round.' 'I hope you're right,' said Lilian doubtfully.

As she had expected, young Tony soon settled in to his new home and responded well to the clear guidelines they had drawn up for the boys. Lilian was an easy-going homely woman and in the coming days was delighted to show off her new charges to all her friends and neighbours. Eli had grown up with the work ethic firmly instilled into him by his father. Hard work brought with it satisfaction in a job well done; approval from one's peers and financial rewards from the boss. He had this in mind when he drew up a list of daily chores for the boys to carry out around the house. In this way he hoped to make them all into a family unit, not just paying war-guests. He realised that they had been running circles around their aunt for some time and getting a lot of their own way. He knew he'd have his work cut out trying to change the negative attitudes of the older boy and he reckoned giving him 'chores' to do wouldn't make this task any easier.

'When I was a lad growing up in a large family back home in England,' he told the boys, 'we didn't have much in the way of money, but we had each other. We pulled our weight around the house and helped out. That's why I want you boys to get used to doing things, like clearing the table, helping Auntie Lil with the washing-up and looking after the dog. It'll be good for you as well as for us!' Tony was eager to please. He wanted to be liked, to be loved, to belong. He would take a while to get the hang of things, but he tried. Godfrey was not so easily won over. He didn't want anyone telling him what to do and when to do it. He dug his heels in and resisted, but Eli had a way of getting folk to do what he wanted them to do and he wasn't going to let a young whipper-snapper get the better of him.

In time Godfrey learned that if he cleared the table and helped with the washing-up without making a fuss, he'd earn a bit of pocket money and be allowed out in the street to play with his new friends.

The Lawrences were close friends with their neighbours the Johns. The relationship was built upon the mutual interest of Mary Johns and Lilian Lawrence in the St. David's United Church Bible class that met every Sunday afternoon In Harvie Avenue and St. Clair Avenue West in Toronto. Tony soon became mates with Don Johns. They were roughly the same age. Pat, Don's sister was a couple of years younger, but tolerated by the boys who didn't usually have much time for girls.

There were a lot of boys living on Latimer and there was always a game or high-jinks going on. Godfrey and Tony had foreign accents and got teased a lot at first, but because they took it all in good part, they were soon accepted like any other kid on Latimer.

Howie Lombard, Doug Hall and Bill Sturtridge were the older boys who ran the Latimer boys gang: Russell Neice, John Huston, Alan Levitt and Don Johns were among the younger members.

Straight away Tony stood out from the crowd being the only kid that had a shock of unruly red hair. The Latimer boys gang were amused to discover that unlike his older brother, Tony was happy to take part in any harum scarum wild game the more mischievous lads could think up. The Spencer boys attended the Allenby elementary school that served the area along with all the other children from Latimer. The school was named after the famous General Allenby who served in World Ward I. It was about four blocks away from Latimer on Avenue Road and Castlefield Avenue. The trip to school on foot gave the lads ample opportunity for snow-ball fights in the winter and the odd skirmish between boys testing their fighting techniques such as boxing, wrestling, tripping each other up and trying to pull each others clothes off in the summer.

When the cry went up, 'C'mon, there's a fight on,' dozens of eager spectators would be drawn to the site of the encounter. There were always one or two 'heavies' who wanted to humiliate a younger weaker boy, but on the whole it was just good-natured fun.

Soon after Tony came to live on Latimer, Don and Tony joined the Scout movement and became cubs. The 151st pack met at Forest Hill United Church once a week from 7 to 8.30 pm. It was a fair old walk down to Bathurst Street During the war, the Cub Master Bill McGill joined the Royal Canadian Air Force and his younger brother took over as 'Akela'. They really enjoyed the competition. Points were awarded for inspection, relay races and badges. They soon accumulated and the winning Six, at the end of each month got to carry the Pack's pennant on their staff.

Sometimes when they were feeling really brave, Don and Tony would come home by going north on Bathurst to Roselawn, then east on Roselawn past the Jewish cemetery to Latimer Avenue. As the street lighting on Roselawn was poor and there were no houses en route, they tended to quicken their pace and break into a run if they heard any strange noises.

But as time went on, Tony became more confident especially with Spot at his side. He would often take the Lawrences black and white fox-haired terrier for a walk up past the Jewish cemetery. It had ceased to hold any terrors for him or so he thought.

Come Halloween, a bunch of his mates decided to have a bit of fun with him. They borrowed some white sheets, covered themselves from head to toe and lay in wait for the unsuspecting pair among the gravestones. When Tony and Spot drew near, all hell broke loose. The gangly ghouls jumped out on them, howling, shrieking and wailing something awful, giving him a terrible fright. He stood rooted to the spot, shivering in his shoes. But his four-legged friend would have none of it. She just went for them, barking and baring her teeth. She tore the sheets off and sent them scarpering like frightened jack rabbits. The spell was broken. Tony fell about laughing his head off.

'That's right, run away you sissies,' he shouted after them, 'frightened of a little dog!' Eventually, tired of the chase, Spot returned to her young master, wagging her tail and jumping up at him. 'Good girl. Good girl, Spot!' he said and gave her a big hug. 'We showed 'em didn't we - bunch of idiots!' She was further rewarded with a couple of her favourite biscuits and the pair ambled home, none the worse for their little Halloween misadventure.

Tony and Godfrey were the only English boys in Allenby. Tony wasn't keen on lessons, like his more academically able brother, but he loved sport. He was a natural where all sports were concerned and this helped his easy integration into a country that placed great emphasis on sporting prowess. Uncle Eli was persuaded to make him some skis and he was soon able to ski to school with his Canadian-born mates.

He palled up with a couple of the older boys, Howie Lombard and Bill Sturtridge. They didn't live far from the golf links and would often explore the surrounding countryside. In the winter it was a favourite place for tobogganing. The bigger boys were always competing, daring one another to take risks. Came the day they decided it was time to test the mettle of their mischievous little friend. 'Betcha you can't go down the hill and stop before the river!' said Howie grinning at Bill.

Tony could see where they were coming from. They were fed up with baiting each other, now it was his turn.

'No, not this time, thank you very much,' he said, bowing out.

They were taken aback, sure that he'd jump at the chance to show off. He was supposed to be the wild kid on their block, ready to do anything. 'What's the matter? Is little Anthony afraid he might fall in the cold river and get a teeny-weeny bit wet?' they goaded him.

'I'm not afraid of anything!' he yelled. 'I'm not afraid of anything!' he yelled louder.

'Did you hear the kid?' said Howie to Bill. 'He's not afraid of anything!' 'I heard him,' said Bill.

'Well, c'mon then Tony, don't just stand there. If you've got the guts get on with it,' they said. Then they waited for some real live action.

But Tony made no move to get on his toboggan and begin the descent. They shrugged their shoulders, looked at him as if he were lower than a guttersnipe and sauntered off. He knew he had to do it or be branded a sissy by all the boys on Latimer. It was a dumb thing to do. He'd been warned time and time again by the Lawrences to keep away from the frozen river. It was treacherous.

'Boys, come back, come back,' he yelled. 'Look, I can do it! I will do it!'

They turned and saw the English kid get on his toboggan, push off and hurtle down the steep hill. He couldn't manage to stop at the bottom, completely missed the bridge and shot out onto the frozen river breaking through the ice and sinking like a stone.

'Great balls of fire!' exclaimed Bill Sturton. Then he and his mate Howie bolted down the hill to the river

'Tony, Tony!' they yelled. 'We'll get yer out. We'll get yer out!

They jumped into the freezing river one after the other and dragged the younger boy out and up onto the bank. They knew the drill. They turned him on his front with his head to one side and pumped his chest up and down, up and down, until he coughed and spluttered and opened his eyes. Then they knew he was going to be all right. Howie heaved a sigh of relief. 'I never want to go through that again,' he said to his mate. 'It was all your fault,' said Bill. 'Well, I did it, didn't I?' said Tony through his chattering teeth.

'You sure did!' they said.

'We'll make a fire and get your wet clothes off before you freeze to death,' said Howie.

They gave him their own jumpers and jackets while they set about trying to dry his clothes, but it proved an abysmal failure. 'We'd better push off,' said Bill. 'This aint working!'

Tony pulled on his wet fire-smoked trousers with great difficulty and put on his frozen jacket and the three slouched off home.

'What on earth have you been up to?' enquired a very cross Lilian Lawrence as she caught Tony in the very act of sneaking in through the back door. 'You've been down to the river! Didn't we tell you, again and again not to go near it. It's dangerous. You could have been drowned! Get those clothes off right away and into a hot bath before you catch your death. Uncle Eli will know of it when he gets in from work and then you'll be for it young man!'

And he was. Eli believed in patiently teaching the boys over and over, but if that didn't work then he fell back on the strap across the backside. He had been taught many a lesson that way himself and sometimes it was the only way.

'Why son, why do you do it when you know it's only going to get you into trouble?' said Eli Lawrence with a sigh. Tony just stood there. There was nothing he could say.

More than anything Tony wanted and needed a Dad. He loved this man who was the only father he'd ever known. This was his home and these good people were his family. Eli Lawrence had called him, 'son' for the first time and the punishment he knew he deserved, didn't hurt a bit, after that.

Anthony & Godfrey Lakeside
Toronto 1941

Auntie Lill & the boys

CHAPTER 6

Unexpected Developments

Life with the Lawrences took on a regular pattern of secure days enabling an upsurge of hope in at least one of the Spencer boys. Sundays were predictable. Auntie Lil and Auntie Mary Johns would accompany Don and Pat Johns and Tony and Godfrey Spencer up to the Forest Hill Church. Their men were not so keen.

Sometimes the children would be allowed to make their own way there, but given this freedom would inevitably arrive late at the church and leave early. Nevertheless there is no doubt that some good came of this regular church-going. In later years, a Presbyterian minister and a staunch young man also valiant for the truth emerged from among their ranks.

The waning of the year was always predictable. Autumn would arrive towards the middle of September shedding abroad all the spilled over splendour of the reddened maple trees. By the end of October, early November, the snow would blow in from the north. It could vary from year to year, but the winter of '42/43 stands out. A heavy fall of snow drifted and completely covered the Lawrences' bungalow.

Tony and Godfrey were soon called upon, like the other boys on Latimer to lend a hand and clear the drive- way. It was hard work, but not only was it fun doing it, but it made them as much a part of that time and place as all the other Canadian boys in the street. That year the snow hung around till March when there was the first sign of spring, but it was still icy well into April.

In the summer the game was baseball. Tony explains it - 'It's a game rather like English rounders, but taken much more seriously. In Canada, it's a man's game. A pitcher throws the ball at the striker. Behind the striker is a catcher. The pitcher has three throws. The striker must hit the ball or run on his third attempt to first base or he is out.' Tony loved the way Canadians were not just spectators, but got stuck in, involved. It meant everything to them. He learnt to swim in Canada too.

Eton Lake in Toronto is shallow one end and deep the other. In the middle of the lake there is a diving platform. One day, Tony was fooling around on the diving board with some of his mates, when he accidentally jumped in on the wrong side. He couldn't swim. 'The lifeguard didn't even get off his backside,' said Tony. 'He just yelled at me when I surfaced - 'Get on your back and kick your legs!' Tony was only a nipper at the time, but that incident made him get down to learning to swim properly; over-arm, the breast stroke, swimming under water. He became a really strong swimmer and is to this day!

Canadian children always looked forward to the long summer holidays spent for the most part in organised camps. Tony and his brother were always separated for the summer holidays. When they were thrown together for any length of time, they would invariably squabble and fight over more or less anything. It was exhausting for the folk around them. The Lawrences thought it best to give them a break from each other and give themselves some breathing space too. It always worked out well. Tony went to Ward Island every summer and Godfrey to Lake Erie. They both had a great time and were ready to start over in the Fall.

Tony wasn't short of pals, but his best buddy was his dog, Spot. She was not really a dog at all, but a bitch, very similar to the English Jack Russell breed, but the height of a small collie. On her white back was a big black spot, hence her name.

During the school term, she would leave the Lawrences' house by knocking open a window and run to meet him at the close of the school day. She was always on time. She never did this at week-ends or during the school holidays. It was as if she knew the times and seasons of the school year. Sometimes she would be allowed to accompany Tony and have the privilege of carrying one of his textbooks in her mouth. He would take the book and say, 'Go on home now Spot. Good girl!' She would put her head on one side as if to plead, 'Let me stay with you today!' but once he repeated the order, she would reluctantly turn and head off home. They were inseparable.

Gladys Butler had been so relieved at the way the boys had settled in with their foster parents. She had not expected it to be such an easy transition. She visited when she could and always made a special effort on their birthdays and at Christmas, but in February '44 she could not make it for Tony's tenth birthday party. She was indisposed. She had been feeling ill for some time and discovered from the medics that she was suffering from 'gall stones' - a very painful condition.

When the boys left her to live with the Lawrences, she had continued to work as a telephonist and live on her own at 1488 King Street, quite comfortably. But when she became indisposed, it soon became apparent that surgery would be necessary. She was unable to work for some time after the operation and began to brood. She missed her people, her country. She longed to get back to good old England.

In 1944, Britain was still in the throes of war with Nazi Germany. Civilians in the capital were being bombarded night and day by 'doodlebugs' - V1s and terrorised by rockets - V2s. But in the safety and security of her life in Canada, Gladys minimised the risk and decided to book passage on the next available boat. Of course, she would also have to take her nephews back to England with her. She was their legal guardian in Canada and there was no question that she would leave them behind.

'Tony, your Aunt Gladys has come to see you,' said an unusually solemn Lilian Lawrence. 'She's got something to tell you.' Tony beamed, not recognizing the sad look in the eyes of his foster Mum.

'Anthony, we're going back to England,' said Gladys Butler fully expecting her good news to be received with whoops of joy from her nephew.

'What?' said a puzzled Tony unable to take in the full import of her 'good' news.

'We're going home. Aren't you pleased?'

'What now?' said Tony in utter disbelief. 'But the war's still on and we're going to stay with Auntie Lil and Uncle Eli until the war's over. That's what you said!'

Gladys turned away from Tony impatiently. She ignored his negative response. She was so excited about the forthcoming journey that she had no idea the devastating effect her plans were to have on the happy ten and a half year old boy who had found his 'home' and his 'family' and wanted no other. Suddenly the awful truth dawned on him.

'It's not fair. I'm not going back,' he blurted out. 'I don't have to, do I Auntie Lil? I want to stay here. I'm not going. I'm not going!'

He looked up at Lilian Lawrence fully expecting her to tell his Aunt Gladys that she had no right to take him back with her to England. But she turned away from him. There were tears in her eyes.

He grabbed his cap and pulled on his coat and ran out of the house swiftly followed by his only faithful friend, Spot. He didn't stop running until he reached one of his gang's hideaways up by the golf links. There was a sharp wind heralding the approach of winter snows. He threw himself down on the hard ground and beat the bare earth with his fists. He cried. He yelled. 'She can't do it, she can't. I won't go. I won't go!'

He frightened poor old Spot. She'd never seen her beloved young master so distressed. She licked his face and gave him her paw.

He tried to figure it out. How could anyone be so powerful that they could spoil another person's life? How was it that children were like possessions to be taken here or there without anyone asking them what they wanted? Aunt Gladys had no right to take him away from the two people who were closer to him than anyone else in the world. He was determined to find a way to stay in the land he had come to think of as his own.

But it was not to be. The boys had to pack up. Lilian and Eli Lawrence couldn't do a thing about it. They loved the boys, but they weren't their legal guardians. They could only bid them a heartbroken farewell and promise to keep in touch.

Tony went over to the Johns house to say his final goodbyes to Don and Pat.

'I'm going to miss you, Tony,' said a tearful Pat. 'I wish you weren't going!'

Don was more circumspect. 'It'll be quite exciting going back home, I guess!' he said.

Tony hugged Spot for the very last time. How could he tell her that she wouldn't be seeing him again for a long time, perhaps never. She wouldn't be able to understand that he wasn't deserting her.

Godfrey took it all in his stride. He wasn't a boy who loved sport and wide open spaces like his younger brother. He'd made the best of it, but he wasn't averse to returning to his home land. In his own quiet way, he found the prospect challenging even exhilarating.

Gladys had always suspected that her nephew Godfrey was sensible, intelligent, accommodating. His positive attitude on this occasion confirmed her in this view. His younger brother was quite different. She found him uncooperative, sullen and rebellious and at times altogether impossible.

Of course, she cared for both her nephews. She would have said that she loved them both equally, but they were growing boys and therefore in need of firm handling. It never even entered her head that they should have a view about their future. It all had to be carefully thought out, planned and executed by responsible adults, caring relatives. She would have been insulted if anyone had tried to point out to her that perhaps she was making the wrong choice for her nephews in seeking to take them back to England while the war was still on and to a mother who would not welcome them.

Tony had ranted and raved, had fought tenaciously for the right to stay in Canada, but having lost the battle, he accepted his Aunt's decision and even looked forward with interest to what he knew would be an exciting sea voyage and to what he hoped would be a bright future.

The trip back was not like the outward voyage. It was a much quicker journey. The RSMS *Bayano*, a Fyffes banana boat (carrying human cargo instead of bananas) joined up with a convoy and as they approached the shores of England, Tony could see lots of ships and an aircraft carrier. Every day they saw double-winged Gladiators fly past at low level. They could even see the pilots who waved a welcome.

Tony had crossed the Atlantic twice and had never disgraced himself by being sea-sick, not like some he could mention. There had been some rough weather too on the outward journey to Canada in 1940. But now as he walked along the railway platform in Liverpool with his brother and his Aunt, he couldn't help himself. He was suddenly as sick as a dog.

Gladys Butler was disgusted with her nephew. He had let her down in public. 'Behave yourself Anthony,' she scolded. 'Remember, you're in England now!' It was late November. The war was in Europe was its sixth year. Everywhere was blacked out. They travelled down to London by train with many stops and starts due to air-raids. On arrival Gladys Butler was anxious to get the boys 'home' as soon as possible. They took a taxi to Watchfield Court flats, Chiswick where she hurriedly offloaded her charges and disappeared.

The boys hadn't seen or heard from their Mother for four and a half years. They felt awkward and didn't know quite what to expect. There were no hugs, no tears of joy, no enquiries about their journey. Nothing was said.

Freda Spencer stood at the kitchen stove cooking a great pile of onions in a big frying-pan as if she was preparing a great banquet for some VIPs who had not yet arrived.

'It seemed very unreal,' said Tony, 'like a bad dream. I'll never forget it. The strong smell of the onions making my eyes water and my Mother totally absorbed in what she was doing seemingly unaware that her two long-lost sons had come home to roost.'

Holiday at Wand Island - Anthony with boat - 1943

Lill & Eli Lawrence

RMS Bayano

CHAPTER 7

Freda

Freda Spencer led a somewhat erratic life. She had only recently learned that her sister Gladys would be returning from Canada with her two nephews in tow. Gladys had assumed that she, being the mother of the boys, would house and care for them.

Freda had never been possessed of homemaking qualities. During the four years that her boys had been war-guests in Canada, her mental and physical health had deteriorated. Her failing mental health was due partly to the devastating effect of losing her employer and close friend, Mr Howard, an American executive of The International Business Machines Company. Mr Howard, his wife and son died when their family home sustained a direct hit from a V1 - a flying enemy bomb.

She had worked on by day, driven an ambulance by night and drowned her sorrows in an alcoholic haze that gave her a permanent hangover. Freda tried to pull herself together when the boys actually appeared at the flat. She had put off thinking about it, half expecting Gladys to change her mind about returning from Canada or hoping that she would find it impossible to get a passage on board ship. After all, the war was still on. She had no right to bring the boys back until it was over. That was the agreement. But here they were. The boys, one aged ten and a half and the other thirteen.

'Well,' said their Mother, looking them up and down. She could hardly recognise them.

'What was it like in Canada then?' she asked Godfrey.

'It was all right,' he replied formally. She tried the same tack with Tony.

'It was great in Canada. I didn't want to come back to England. In any case the war is still on isn't it?'

'Yes,' she replied wearily, 'the war is still on.' She looked at her sons and saw strangers. Strangers who had come to stay at an inconvenient time. 'I suppose you'd better put your things in the bedroom. My lodger, George Page sleeps in there. You and George will have to share the bed, Godfrey,' she said.

'Where will I sleep?' enquired Tony.

Freda frowned. She hadn't had time to think about it. Where they would sleep. She slept in the blue velvet arm chair in the lounge. She had an irritating cough that was worse at night and kept her awake. It was quite a big lounge. She'd have to make him up a bed on the floor near the radiator. The nights were cold in London in November, cold and miserable.

There was no time for any more small talk. An air- raid warning was filling the air with its high-pitched whining, startling the boys. As it faded away, they could hear the ack-ack guns sounding off at enemy targets overhead. Then there was a loud bang, swiftly followed by another. The war was still going on! They could hear it, smell it, feel it all around them. What were they supposed to do? Where could they go?

'Don't worry. It'll be over soon,' Freda said. She lit up a cigarette and poured herself a whiskey. 'Don't you ever go to a shelter or anything?' enquired Godfrey not at all reassured by her casual attitude. Everything in the flat was shaking violently with each resounding bang.

'I used to go to a shelter, but it takes some time to get down to it from here. It's usually all over by the time you get down the stairs. There isn't any point!'

The boys huddled together under the dining table, putting their fingers in their ears to dull the noise and the rising panic they were feeling. Eventually the 'all-clear' was sounded and they made a bee-line for the toilet, Tony getting there first.

'What do you kids want to eat? I expect you're starving?' Freda called after them.

'No, I'm not hungry,' said Godfrey, 'He still felt as if he was going to be sick and looked as white as a sheet.

'I am!' said Tony. Tony was a growing lad and was always hungry.'

'Well, let's see. What have I got to go with the onions I've been frying? I managed to get some sausages. Filled with sawdust, I expect,' Freda quipped.

'Sawdust,' said Tony, 'what's sawdust?'

'It's only meant to be a joke, silly,' said his mother.

Later they both went to the bathroom just to get away from their Mother. They could not help recognising that she was ill. She was smoking all the time, yet she had a bad cough. They looked at the grey walls, the chipped enamel bath and then at each other, trying to make sense of the impossible situation in which they found themselves. Tony opened his mouth to complain, but Godfrey beat him to it. 'Don't you start!' he said angrily.

'I never said anything,' said Tony sullenly.

'You'd better not,' said Godfrey.

'It's not my fault,' said Tony. 'I just want to go back to Auntie Lil and Uncle Eli.'

'Well, you can't, so shut-up about it!' said Godfrey.

They were summoned to meet their Mother's lodger, George. A tall tired looking man who said, 'Hello,' sat down and began reading his copy of the EVENING STANDARD. He ate his meal in silence, excused himself and went to his room. Tony and Godfrey were disappointed. He hadn't even been polite enough to enquire about their trip over from Canada. Tony discounted him right away, but Godfrey couldn't afford to be so dismissive. He would soon be sharing a room with this stranger and what was even worse, the same bed.

As the days passed, Tony found that his questions got on his mother's nerves. Godfrey saw the signs and took himself off to the local library. Tony didn't have the sense to keep his unhappiness at having to leave Canada to himself. He drove Freda to distraction.

'Oh stop going on and on about it,' she said. 'Get into the kitchen and wash-up. Make yourself useful, for God's sake!'

Tony's bed space under the old bulbous radiator which was supposed to be only a temporary measure, became the only place he had to call his own. He felt worse off than any pet dog. He was certainly worse off than Spot - the pet dog he had been forced to leave behind in Canada. He brooded over his dramatically changed life and grew more miserable by the day.

He couldn't stop picking rows with his mother, goading her, pricking her conscience and forcing her to answer his endless complaints

'Do you think that I asked for you to come back?' she hurled at him one day when she was fed up to the teeth with his constant moans. 'I never wanted to set eyes on you again. You should have stayed there while you had the chance. There's nothing here for you, nothing!'

She would send Tony out to the local shops with a long list just to get rid of him for an hour or two. There was still rationing in Britain and Tony had no idea how the system worked. People in the shops looked puzzled when he asked for goods and made it obvious that he couldn't add up the change. He was big enough to know better, they thought. He spoke with a funny accent too, like a foreigner, like the Yanks. Perhaps his Dad was a Yank. Some believed that he and his Mum had been left behind when his old man had hooked it back home to America. That had happened to a lot of young girls. They knew all about it.

Tony was used to Canadian dollars and the metric system. He had no idea that a pound sterling was equal to two hundred and forty pence. That a 'bob' was a shilling and a 'tanner' sixpence. It was always worse when he got home. He never managed to get everything on the list and the change he brought back was always wrong.

'You're an idiot,' she hurled at him one day after he'd been shopping.

'I'm not. I'm not,' he shouted back. 'I don't understand the money here. It's not the same as in Canada.'

'If you mention, 'Canada' just one more time, I swear I'll give you such a good hiding you'll never forget it,' Freda promised him.

'If you don't want me, then why can't I go back to Auntie Lil and Uncle Eli?' Tony pleaded. 'They wanted me. They didn't hate me, like you do!'

That was it. Freda lashed out at him again and again. She was landed with him. She couldn't send him back to Canada. She would gladly have put him on the next boat to China if she could. She only wanted him to give it a rest, but the little fool couldn't keep his mouth shut.

Godfrey had found out about the local schools on his visits to the library and persuaded his mother to let him and his brother go. She hadn't even thought that they missed school. Most children hated going to school. Tony started going with his brother, but he didn't get on well with other kids who made fun of him, so gave it up as a bad job. His mother wasn't a bit surprised when he dropped out of school. She'd always told him that he was never going to amount to anything.

Freda had been on sick leave and instructed by her doctor to take it easy and rest. She found no rest at all in the flat, so she signed herself off at her doctor's surgery.

She devised a cunning plan to keep her youngest son out of mischief while she was at work on the one hand and to punish him for his persistent rudeness and insolence on the other. Before leaving for work on Monday morning, she locked Tony into the bathroom to tackle a bath full of dirty washing. A packet of blue washing crystals was supposed to make the job as easy as falling off a log. 'The handkerchiefs were the worse,' Tony remembers. 'They were horrible - wet and slimy.'

At first he thought of it as a game. He amused himself by taking off his shoes and trousers, getting into the bath and jumping up and down on the wet clothes and singing out loud and clear:

'This is the way we wash the clothes, Wash the clothes, Wash the clothes. This is the way we wash the clothes On a wet and windy morning!'

In this way he managed to leave more water on the floor than there was in the bath. But when he had exhausted all his watery ideas, he yelled and screeched, jumped out of the bath and kicked the bathroom door, again and again. All to no avail. It proved to be a miserable long day.

His brother came into the flat first and let him out. He was starving hungry. He quickly made himself a bread and dripping sandwich, devoured it and followed that with more bread and a scraping of jam. Then he washed it down with buckets of cold clear water. He only had bad things to say about his mother.

'She's a wicked witch! A bat! An ugly Monster and I hate her! I hate her! I hate her!' 'If you go on like that when she comes home, she'll do it again,' warned his brother.

'No, I'll keep as quiet as a mouse,' said Tony.

But Tony did not keep as quiet as a mouse, so next day found him back in the bathroom and once again the door was locked. At first he just sat down on the floor, folded his arms across his chest and felt very sorry for himself. But he soon got bored with doing nothing. He looked around for some way out. The window, he opened it and looked out. Right next door was a drainpipe. Soon he was shinning down it to freedom.

He ran and ran until he found some swings and roundabouts in a park and spent a good time there. He only moved on when his stomach growled reminding him that he had missed breakfast. He was attracted by the enticing smell of cooking meat to a street trader selling hot-dogs. He hung about until there was a lull in trade.

'You hungry or something kid?' asked the trader.

'Yes,' said Tony, 'but I haven't got any money.'

'Here, have this one on me,' he said, handing him a scrumptious hot-dog. 'I was a hungry kid like you not so long ago!

He was happy to wander up and down the streets of London, until the light began to fade. Then he saw kids pouring out of schools and decided it was time for him to make his way home. He climbed back up the drainpipe leading to his mother's bathroom passing the open window of the tenants who lived underneath. On the window ledge was a sight for sore eyes. A piping hot dinner left there to cool. His luck was definitely in today, he thought. As quick as a flash he transferred the plate to the window ledge above. He nipped smartly into the bathroom, gobbled down the meat and two veg, washed the plate and in double quick time replaced it.

Later, afraid of the consequences should he be found out, he mentioned the incident to his brother. Godfrey was able to reassure him. 'A copper lives underneath our flat,' he said. 'But he won't dare report you because he's living in sin!' Tony had no idea what 'living in sin' was all about, but he stopped worrying.

It was Good Friday. His mother was home from work, but it wasn't long before she was finding fault with her youngest son. He responded to a hit around the head by taking one of her brass plates displayed in a bracket on the lounge wall and hurling it at her.

It missed its target and went sailing out of an open window. Then he threw two more. His mother put a stop to his antics by landing him a heavy blow to the side of his head and knocking him down. He scrambled to his feet and made a dash for the door.

'You'd better bring those plates back here or you'll be in trouble,' she shouted after him.

He found them. One was bent, the others were buckled. He reluctantly retraced his steps and put the damaged plates on the dining table.

'Look what you've done,' cried his mother hysterically. 'Get out! get out! and don't come back! Do you hear me?' Yes, he had heard. He ran off, not knowing where he was going, but sure of one thing - he was never ever going back.

*Freda Spencer - Anthony &
Godfrey's mother*

The Spencer boys father

CHAPTER 8

Godfrey Spencer

Godfrey Spencer was sitting in an armchair, his head bent over a book. He could lose himself in this way and successfully block out all that was going on around him. He was surprised when his mother burst into the bedroom he shared with Mr Page and yelled at him:

'And what d'you think you're doing, you lazy good-for-nothing!'

'I'm reading,' he replied lamely.

'Reading, reading, that's all you're good for!'

'What's the matter?' he enquired at a loss to know what he had done to make her so irritable.

'It's that stupid brother of yours. He's run off again. He's such a handful. I can't take much more of this Godfrey. You'd better go and find him.'

Godfrey reluctantly closed his book, went into the kitchen, grabbed whatever was to hand to eat and left the flat. He was seriously fed up with his younger brother. It seemed to him that Anthony goaded their mother until she felt compelled to hit him. He had reasoned with him time and time again not to argue because it only made her angry.

He knew that his mother had no idea how to look after him and his brother, but he felt that she was the injured party. Their father had left her in the lurch. He was the one to be blamed for her drinking. He would never forgive his father for deserting their mother and his two sons.

He didn't argue with Freda and he got on well with her partner, George. He was suitably impressed when George claimed to have designed the famous 'Mae West' lifesaving jacket that had saved thousands of lives. He also discovered that he had been married before he met Freda and had two grown up sons who were serving in the Royal Navy overseas.

Godfrey went first of all to Turnham Green, one of Tony's favourite haunts, but he wasn't anywhere to be seen. He made his way to Chiswick Common, but drew a blank there as well. He returned home more than irritated with his brother for wasting his time and being a rotten nuisance. Perhaps he was already at home, he thought.

Freda was getting ready to go out when he arrived back at the flat. She seemed in a better mood. Mr Page was taking her out to have a drink at one of the local pubs.

'Don't wait up,' she said. 'I expect we'll be late.'

She hadn't even enquired about Anthony and his whereabouts. But the next morning there was all hell to play.

'Where is he, where is he?' Freda shouted at Godfrey. Didn't I tell you to find him and bring him back?'

'I looked everywhere, but I couldn't find him,' he said. 'It's not my fault.'

Freda wasn't feeling at all well after a night out on the tiles. 'Oh, you're just as bad as your stupid brother. You're a pair of idiots, useless - no good, like your no-good father! Are you listening to me?'

At last the quietly spoken Godfrey was shaken. He could not stand for this, even from his mother. 'Don't talk like that mother. We don't deserve it.

It's not our fault our father left you. We didn't ask to be born. We didn't have a choice, did we?'

'How dare you talk to me like that!' said Freda. She approached

61

him with a raised hand and brought it down hard on his face, again and again. 'You boys have no respect, no respect at all for your elders. What did they teach you out there in your precious Canada? You haven't got the manners of a pig!' and she went for him again.

'No wonder Anthony is so miserable here,' said Godfrey. 'You've been making his life hell!'

'Well, well, standing up for our little brother now are we? Don't bother. You're a weakling, a snivelling little coward. You can't even stand up for yourself!'

Godfrey looked over at Mr Page expecting him to say something, anything in his defence. But he showed no sign of being at all interested in what was going on between him and his mother. He had thought that they were friends. Sadly he realised that he had been mistaken.

'As for your brother,' continued Freda angrily, 'I don't care if he never comes back. Good riddance, is what I say. Good riddance to bad rubbish!'

At this awful remark, George Page did try to intervene.

'Come on Freda, that's a bit hard!' he said.

She swung round and confronted her lodger. 'And you can mind your own business!' she shouted at him.

Godfrey retreated to the kitchen to peel potatoes, his usual chore, and left them to it. He heard them arguing. Freda wasn't the only one who was angry. Godfrey was furious, but it had the effect of making him use the potato peeling task to bring his anger under control. He was determined whatever his mother said or did, he was going to remain icy cool and calm. Eventually his mother joined him in the kitchen and began cooking the Sunday lunch without saying another word.

On Easter Monday morning, George Page shook Godfrey awake.

'Godfrey, I'm worried about Anthony,' he said.

Not before time, thought Godfrey.

'He's been out for three nights. He must be sleeping rough

somewhere. Can't you think of any place he could be?'

He shrugged his shoulders, got out of bed and went to the bathroom. At last somebody cared about what was happening to his brother. He washed and went back to the bedroom to get dressed.

'After breakfast, I'll go out again and see if I can find him,' he said. 'He won't be able to stay out much longer. He hasn't got any money on him. He'll be starving hungry.'

'Your mother has a terrible headache this morning,' said George. 'You'd better make yourself scarce.'

Godfrey could take a hint. It wasn't long before he was off accepting a half-a-crown from George to get himself and Anthony, if he could find him, something to eat.

At first he didn't have a clue where to look for his brother, but suddenly it dawned upon him where Anthony could be - Kew Gardens. They'd gone there from time to time just for a lark. On one occasion, Anthony had hidden in one of the many gardener's potting sheds, making it almost impossible for Godfrey to find him. Kew Gardens was a big place, much the worse for wear due to bomb damage, but easy for kids to go in and out without much trouble. He felt confident about his hunch and bought some breakfast sausage sandwiches and a big bottle of Tizer to share with his brother as soon as he found him.

Godfrey took a short cut through the back streets of Chiswick diving in and out of deserted and derelict houses, just in case Anthony had taken this route and might possibly be on his way back. Then he was in luck. He saw him going over Kew Bridge. He called out, 'Anthony! Anthony!' But he hadn't heard. He kept on going.

He was quite out of breath when he managed at last to catch up with him.

'Anthony wait a minute! Where on earth have you been? I've been looking for you everywhere,' he said.

'What for?' said Anthony sullenly. 'I'm not going back. I'm never going back!'

'Look, I've brought you a sandwich and some Tizer.'

That was different. Anthony perked up. Food was always good news. He ate one of the sandwiches and drank some of the Tizer and then he grinned. What a rascal, thought his brother, what a cheeky rascal.

'What have you been doing for food?' asked Godfrey.

'I found a nice potting shed in Kew Gardens,' said Anthony. 'I go there to sleep at night. One of the old gardener's has been leaving me food. It's been all right. A lot better than sleeping back in the flat underneath that rotten noisy radiator!'

'What have you been getting up to during the day?' Godfrey asked.

'I've just been wandering about. Nobody's been bothering me. Some of the street traders have been giving me a free hand-out now and again. I'm never going back. Mother can't stand the sight of me. She's always bashing me and shouting her head off. I can't go back there.' But in spite of his bravado, his voice broke and he had a job to stop himself from bawling. 'What are we going to do Godfrey?' he said.

'I don't know, but you can't go on living like an old tramp. You're only a kid!' said his brother.

'Come on, show me your hideout,' said Godfrey endeavouring to bring back that cheeky grin to his brother's face.

'Here we are,' said Anthony. 'What do you think of it?' There were old overcoats hanging behind the door; a makeshift seat made out of a plank of wood supported by two wooden grates. The usual garden implements - a spade and a fork. There was an old pair of boots on the floor and pots of all sizes.

It seemed pretty dire as a place to sleep in to Godfrey, but he nodded and said, 'Yeah, it's a great den.'

'I've got something to tell you,' said Tony, 'but you must promise not to tell anyone.'

'What's that then?' queried an anxious Godfrey.

'Something mighty powerful has happened to me since I ran away and came here,' he said mysteriously. 'You know that pagoda out there in the Gardens?'

'Yes,' replied Godfrey puzzled. On one of his visits he had read the plaque attached to the pagoda that stated it had been designed by a certain Englishman, William Chambers who had been fascinated by eastern culture. 'Well,' continued Tony lowering his voice, 'one day I was just standing in front of it and looking up at it and it happened.' 'What?' said Godfrey.

'It seemed the most important building in the whole world and sort of 'alive', if you know what I mean. It was so strong and powerful, I knew that nothing and no-one - not even Hitler's doodlebugs could ever even touch it. I stood up straight to attention, saluted it and said out loud so that the pagoda could hear me:

'I will never ever drink alcohol, as long as I live! It was amazing Godfrey! I'd made a vow to it and it seemed to say, not with words, but like something I heard inside myself, 'Yes, I've heard your vow.'

Godfrey was stunned by his brother's admission. He was afraid that he'd gone right off his head, but he was careful not to show that he had any doubts about the amazing 'experience'. He was convinced that it was imperative that he persuade his brother to return with him to the flat that night.

The Spencer brothers arrived back at the flat decidedly apprehensive. In their absence Freda Spencer had made up her mind what she intended to do with her ill-mannered, uncontrollable, ungrateful and sadly it must be said, unwanted rebellious boys.

They were greeted by George who let them in and then broke the news.

'Your mother has just popped out for a bit,' he said, a trifle embarrassed, 'but she left word that if you both turned up, you were to pack up all your things, have a bath and get to bed. She's taking you to stay with your Aunt Sylvia first thing in the morning - for a bit of a holiday!' Godfrey was relieved. At least Anthony wasn't going to get a beating!

The next morning Freda, tight-lipped and straight-faced bundled the boys and their luggage onto a bus and in strained silence they travelled to their Aunt's house.

Aunt Sylvia was not pleased to see them. She left the boys in the kitchen eating biscuits and drinking cocoa while she and her sister Freda had angry words about the boys in the hallway. She had not been informed that they were coming. She would certainly have prevented it.

'I'm a district midwife, for God's sake, not a child minder!' she shouted at her sister. 'I can't have boys staying here! I hold clinics every day for pregnant women. Don't you understand Freda, it's just impossible!' This tense exchange was suddenly interrupted by a loud urgent knock at the door. Sylvia opened it. As if to prove her point, a heavily pregnant lady was huffing and puffing on her doorstep, seeking her help. She took her through to her consulting room and made her comfortable. This was Freda's chance to make a run for it. Sylvia wasn't born yesterday. She knew that Freda had no intention of taking her boys back after a week or two or ever. She was landed with them. They weren't bad boys, they were just unfortunate to have a bad mother. She'd have them for a while, but she couldn't possibly offer them a permanent home. She would enlist her sister Gladys' help.

Gladys felt the only solution would be for the boys to be placed in an orphanage, so she wrote to Fegan's Home for Boys about their unhappy plight. The boys didn't know it, but they were about to be catapulted out of the frying-pan into a blazing fiery furnace.

CHAPTER 9

'Bleak House'

It was June, 1945. The war in Europe was over, but ration books, clothing coupons and identity cards were still a requirement on being admitted to Fegan's Home for Boys together with a medical form signed by a doctor. Mr N.E. Bennett, the General Superintendent, personally interviewed the boys seeking admission to ensure that they were fit to commence the arduous training that all the boys in Fegan's underwent.

'Welcome to Fegan's. I'm Mrs Bennett,' said a little lady with a strong Scottish accent.

The Spencer boys had no luggage with them. In fact the clothes they were wearing, including their highly polished shoes would be taken away by their Aunt when she left. The boys would never wear them again. They were passed on to the Salvation Army.

Gladys Butler was taken by Mrs Bennett on a grand tour of the Stony Stratford building, including the dormitories, the dining room, the chapel and the school. She was eager to point out that all the boys in Fegan's received an elementary education.

In the meantime the new boys were issued with Fegan's dark grey uniform which included the notorious 'itchy' shirts. None of the boys wore long trousers at Stony, even if they reached the manly height of six feet!

Anthony was to be known in Fegan's from that day forward as 'Spencer 50' and his brother Godfrey, 'Spencer 62'. Both boys had been tubbed and scrubbed prior to leaving London early that morning, but they were still obliged to have the compulsory 'admission bath'. Then their clothes were taken away and given to their Aunt.

'Goodbye, boys,' said their Aunt Gladys. 'Don't forget to write. Auntie Sylvia and I will try to get down to see you when we can.'

The boys stood there stiffly in their prison-grey uniforms looking awkward and embarrassed. Inside their 'itchy' grey shirts their hearts were pounding. Now they knew what unwanted pets must feel like when admitted to Battersea Dogs' Home - utterly wretched and miserable!

Gladys Butler turned to Mrs Bennett. 'Anthony's the mischievous one,' she said. 'You'll need to keep a good eye on him.' Then she turned back to her nephew and said; 'Behave yourself Anthony. Always do as you're told and you'll get along all right'. It was probably good advice, but on that day and in that unsympathetic setting, it fell on stony ground.

She turned her attention to Godfrey. He looked back at her with unveiled reproach in his eyes, but she did not see it. She smiled at him. 'You're going to make yourself useful aren't you Godfrey and look after your little brother?' Godfrey made no reply, but Tony was affronted. He very much resented being constantly labelled, 'Godfrey's little brother!' It was as if he had no separate identity and would forever have to play that inferior role.

Then she was gone. She was not an uncaring Aunt. She always did what she could for Freda's boisterous boys, but she resented being the one who took responsibility for them. She didn't know it, but she lacked warmth and tenderness. She couldn't see that the boys needed anything more than a roof over their heads, food in their stomachs and strict overseers to make sure they kept out of Trouble.

Tony hung his head down. He wondered what on earth he was doing there. It was for orphans. He wasn't an orphan. Orphans were children whose mothers and fathers had died and gone to heaven.

His mother was ill and in hospital, but she was still alive. He couldn't understand why his Aunt hadn't contacted their father. He was sure that if she had done so, he and his brother wouldn't have been placed in an orphanage. He had asked her again just before they left London that morning.

'Your father, Anthony, didn't lift a finger to help you when you were born,' she had said, 'so what makes you think he'd do anything for you now?'

'He sends money to help pay for our keep, doesn't he? That's doing something! He's my father and I want to see him!'

'This painful subject is closed, Anthony. Your Aunt Sylvia and I will do what is best for you as always!'

Seated on the train taking her back to Euston, Gladys Butler reflected on the unhappy circumstance that had necessitated placing her nephews in Fegan's. She blamed her sister Freda for being feckless; for having a nervous breakdown and for being unwilling as well as unable to look after her own progeny. It had upset her to leave them behind in that austere place, but she couldn't take them in. She was only renting rooms herself and her sister Sylvia worked all the hours that God sent as a District Midwife. She sighed and put the whole sorry business out of her mind. She was tired. After all it had been a very long day.

Meanwhile, back in the Orphanage at Stony Stratford, the new boys were being bombarded with questions by old boys in the dormitory where they had been allotted a bed and a wooden box in which to store their 'Sunday' clothes.

'What's yer name? Where do yer come from? Are you orphans? Who was that lady who brought you in? Will she be sending you food parcels? You'll be needing them in 'ere!'

Tony was full of bitterness. He didn't like the boys crowding around and bothering him. He was determined not to answer any of their stupid questions. He was afraid that if they kept pestering him, he'd make an ass of himself and start bawling. He knew that would be unforgivable in an eleven year old boy, even if his world was falling apart. He shot his interrogators angry looks, but said nothing. This unfriendly reaction made them shrug their shoulders and give him a wide berth.

The older boys quizzed Godfrey. He told them with some pride that he was thirteen and a half. He was not overawed by them or intimidated by their invitations to prove that he could fight.

'I bet you can't fight. I bet you can't fight as good as Smithy. He's taller and stronger than you. He could knock you down easy!'

Spencer 62 didn't show any sign of fear or interest. He told them calmly that he could fight - if he had to. Yes, he played football and cricket and yes, he would share a food parcel if his Aunts sent him any. That was all they wanted to know. He was in. He was all right.

But Spencer 50 was not all right. That night he tossed and turned and couldn't get off to sleep. He was anxious, nervous, fearful. Finally he attempted to get out of bed. He wanted a drink. The boy in the next bed whispered, 'You mustn't get out of bed after lights out. It's against the Rules mate!'

'But I need to go to the bathroom,' he said.

'Shut up will yer or you'll get us all into Trouble. There's no talking allowed in the dorm after lights out!'

Tony reluctantly got back into bed. He dozed on and off until he was rudely awakened by the ringing of a very loud bell. It was 6.30 a.m. He sat up. All the other boys in the dorm knew what to do and where to go. They took their towels and soap and scurried like soldier ants downstairs to the bathroom for their regulation daily 'strip wash'.

'Come on mate. Don't hang about,' shouted one of the bigger boys. 'Get your soap and towel and follow the others pronto!' Tony forced himself to follow the crowd.

After their strip wash and inspection it was time for breakfast. Breakfast at Fegan's was a jolly way to start the day. It comprised two slices of bread and margarine followed by a bowl of cold lumpy porridge. To round off this hearty meal there was always a mug of cold watery cocoa.

Following this substantial repast, the place became a hive of industry. One hundred and eighty boys set about performing their assigned tasks. They made beds, tidied their dormitory, washed up the breakfast things, scrubbed and polished floors, cleaned bathrooms, sinks and lavatories, swept the parade ground and miraculously managed to get all this work done before 9.00 a.m. when the clanging of a bell sounded indicating that it was time for school.

But Tony being a new boy was taken to the Boot Room by his house master. He was informed that all the boys had to clean their hobnailed boots every day, but only in the Boot Room. Tony set to work cleaning his boots which already appeared clean to his untrained eye. An hour or so later when he had polished his boots so that his master could see his handsome face reflected in the dazzling shine, he was sent on an errand to the office.

'Go down the long passage and you'll find a door at the end,' he said. 'Go through that door and you'll find the store room and next to that is the office. Give this note to the lady you'll find in there. She'll tell you what to do. All right then, off you go Spencer 50!'

Tony was more than a bit overawed by the bigness of the Home which had so many rooms and corridors, but he started off boldly enough. He found the long passageway and walked down it until he came to the last door. He opened it hopefully, but was bewildered to find that the door led on to the street outside the main gates of the Home. Standing on the pavement talking to a posh-looking lady was none other than the General Superintendent himself, Mr Norman Bennett.

'What are you doing out here boy!' he enquired of Spencer 50 angrily. 'Are you thinking of running away?'

'Tony was stupefied, dumbstruck. Mr Bennett was an enormous man, stern, straight-faced with white hair and a greying walrus moustache. He was a formidable frightening giant to a new boy who had inadvertently lost his way.

'Go straight to Sick Bay and wait for me there. Do you hear me, boy?' he yelled.

'Yes sir,' Tony managed to blurt out. He turned on his heel, retraced his steps and had to ask another boy for directions. He had yet to learn that the Dispensary was also known as the Sick Bay and many a boy who had visited it feeling a bit under the weather, left it feeling as sick as a parrot.

After what seemed a day and a night, Mr Bennett walked in through the door and shut it firmly behind him. He took a leather strap from a hook on the wall and turned to the waiting boy and said: You're one of the new boys aren't you?'

'Yes sir, Spencer 50,' Tony replied.

'Well, Spencer 50, this is how we deal with deceitful and disobedient boys here at Stony. Take your trousers down and bend over this chair.'

'But sir, I...'

'Bend over and stop blabbering,' demanded the Superintendent.

Spencer 50 bent over the chair and was given six of the best on his bare buttocks. He couldn't believe it. He hadn't done anything to deserve it. He was very angry, outraged, but determined not to cry out whatever happened. No longer afraid, he just despised this great big bully. 'Let that be a lesson to you!' said his unjust taskmaster doubting that it would be and fully expecting to see the wretched boy again under similar circumstances in the not too distant future.

'Go and join the boys in the long passage and start scrubbing the tiles on the floor. I'll come along shortly and make sure you've done the job properly. Is that clear, Spencer 50?'

'Perfectly sir,' replied Tony.

'Well, don't just stand there like an idiot. Go and get on with it!'

This was Spencer 50s introduction to the harsh regime that was then in place in Fegan's Home for Boys. He wondered how he or indeed any boy would ever be able to survive it.

Fegans Homes

Chapter 10

Hard Times

Spencer 50 soon learned the daily routine at Fegan's and reluctantly got on with it. All the hundred and eighty boys were kept usefully occupied every minute of every day and night. Talking after lights out was a Punishable Offence. Once in bed, we were not allowed to go out to the toilet or to get a drink. It was a Punishable Offence. No. 50 was to learn that more or less everything at Fegan's was a Punishable Offence. The place was run on strictly negative lines. Punishments were given for not washing properly, not making one's bed properly, not keeping clean and tidy and of course for Insolence (which at Fegan's meant taking during meal times). The boys were employed in keeping the Home and grounds in good order as there was precious little paid help.

The Spencer boys could not help noticing after a month or two had elapsed that nothing ever varied at Fegan's. None of the boys had to wonder what would be on the menu for Mondays. It was always rissoles; Tuesdays, stew; Wednesdays, pease pudding and so on. Once or twice a week the second course at mid-day would consist of small suet puddings that the boys called, 'baby heads' covered with treacle. This should have been a treat, but the treacle was so diluted with water to make it go further that in the end it didn't taste anything like treacle.

There were no paid cleaners, stokers or kitchen hands. The work was done by the boys themselves. This meant that they were the ones who swept the parade ground and scrubbed and polished the floors. Some boys were more likely to be found scrubbing and polishing than others such as Spencer 50.

'What time do yer call this No.50. You're late for breakfast again!' said the Duty Master looking at his pocket watch.

'It's not my fault,' Spencer 50 replied unapologetically. 'One of the boys in my dorm messed up my bed and I had to stay behind and make it all over again.'

'Is that so,' said the Duty Master. 'Well now that is a shame because you'll have to report for scrubbing duty in the long passage after breakfast!'

'It isn't fair!' protested No.50. 'I'm always being picked on.'

'Right! Now you're being insolent. Report to the Dispensary before doing the scrubbing duty.'

'But sir,' began Tony about to protest further at this incomprehensible injustice.

'Are you still arguing with me No.50? enquired the red-faced angry master?

No.50 sighed, 'No, sir.'

'You'll get on much better No.50 if you learn to keep your mouth shut and just do as you are told. Do I make myself clear?'

'Yes sir,' replied a temporarily defeated Tony, lowering his eyes and staring sullenly at the quarry tiles on the Dining Hall floor.

No.50 was destined to learn everything in Fegan's the hard say. But, in spite of repeated punishments, he could not manage to stay out of trouble. He didn't know how to keep his head down. In any case his unruly red hair didn't do much to help matters. He stood out from the crowd and spoiled the view of mousy brown-haired conformity. He never undertook his duties with the required liveliness and enthusiasm expected of all Fegan Boys and what is more, he gave the impression of being uncooperative and even, dare I say it, of being downright rebellious. Therefore, he was often to be found on his knees scrubbing tiles in the Dining Hall or similarly employed in the long - two hundred and forty yards long - passageway. Over the years he came to know the size, the pattern formation and the colour of those tiles and can still accurately describe them decades later.

On one of these occasions, he was on his way to collect a scrubbing brush, a pail of water, a block of soap and a floor cloth when he happened to meet up with Spencer No.62.

'On punishment duty again Anthony?' said his brother lightly.

'Yes and it isn't fair!' said Tony. 'Of course you never have to do any scrubbing. I hate this place!'

'You always were a miserable wretch Anthony. Just stop whinging and putting everyone's back up. It won't last forever!'

'I'm not so sure about that,' said Tony gloomily as he joined the other unfortunates scrubbing their ten punishment tiles that day.

Things began to improve for No.50 when he joined the choir. Stony Stratford had its own chapel, organ, bellow and choir master, 'Dad' Swell. It had a pulpit for visiting preachers and a congregation made up of outside folk - village people.

The only time boys went outside the Home was on Sunday afternoons. They were taken for a walk in crocodile fashion to one of the surrounding villages and back home for tea. The local children would see them on their way back to Fegan's and call after them - 'Hey, orphan boys. Where's your ma? Where's your da?' They would laugh and jeer at the poor boys dressed in their workhouse grey uniforms and so enjoyed their discomfort that they made it a regular Sunday afternoon pastime. They were careful to keep their distance though, just in case the orphans broke ranks and came after them. Their heavy hob-nailed boots looked as if they could inflict more than a bit of damage if it came to a fight.

The Fegan boys were in a fix. They were straining at the bit to have a go at the locals and show them what they were made of, but the prospect of meeting up with the Superintendent and his leather strap as soon as they returned to the Home, tempered their enthusiasm for a bust-up. And being grown lads and always hungry put the lid on it. It would no doubt have meant reduced rations and hard labour for a week and no pocket money for a month. No village kid, however big-mouthed was worth it.

The funny thing is that most of the kids together with their mothers and grannies, were often in the congregation at Fegan's on Sunday evenings looking as innocent as new-born lambs and joining heartily in the singing of the hymns as if their hearts and souls were full of pentecostal fire. Tony couldn't understand it.

He made friends with a boy in the choir called David Kent. He was gifted musically and given the opportunity of learning to play an instrument of his choice. Tony confided in his new mate that he really wanted to learn to play the violin. He put in a request for lessons time and time again, but was turned down. Nevertheless he enjoyed being in the choir and was delighted when chosen to understudy Tony Motrom who was to be the soloist at the forthcoming Annual Fegan's Reunion to be held at the Central Hall, Westminster, London.

The choir of sixty boys practised and worked hard in the months leading up to the Reunion. Tony wrote to his Aunts Gladys and Sylvia telling them about it and received a letter back assuring him of their attendance.

At last the longed for day arrived and the choir boys with their choir master, 'Dad' Swell, were bussed up to London for the big event. Tony remembers the choir singing the hymn, 'There is a green hill far away,' when unfortunately Tony Motrom's voice 'broke'. There was consternation in the ranks. The choir master hurriedly turned to Spencer 50 and said: 'You'll have to sing the solo. Give it your best No.50!' Tony was thrilled. He had got his chance to shine.

He scanned the invited congregation seated in the balcony and soon found his Aunt Sylvia and her companion Auntie Emily, but no Aunt Gladys. His eyes chanced to alight on his mother sitting alongside them only a few yards from where he was standing. He was so proud to think that she had come to hear him sing. He looked eagerly towards her hoping to catch her eye, but she appeared restless, distressed as if she were only there under sufferance. There was no sign of recognition when she turned her head and looked at him. He sang his solo, but it had upset him to see his mother. It brought back a flood of unhappy memories. Later he returned to the Home miserable and wretched.

CHAPTER 11

Winds of Change

'Mr George', as he became known to the boys in Fegan's was an ex-Indian Army sergeant. The boys soon learned that if they misbehaved they would be punished, but they also learned that he was fair. This was very important to Spencer 50. In that first awful year at Fegan's he trusted none of the staff, but with the coming of 'Mr George', this longing for justice and fairness was met in the way he dealt with the boys.

'He cared for the boys,' said Tony. If you fell and cut your knee in the playground, he would see to it that you were o.k. He was strict and if he caught you misbehaving you were punished, but he was consistent. He was fair and he didn't have favourites.'

Godfrey Spencer remembers Mr George introducing himself to the boys in the Dining Hall during the School holidays in 1946. 'He had a whistle, like a referee's whistle and he made it abundantly clear that when he blew that whistle wherever you were and whatever you were doing, you stopped - frozen to the spot and were absolutely quiet unless you wanted the dubious privilege of coke crushing or quarry tile scrubbing.

But there was another side to him,' said Godfrey. 'On his day off, he would take two or three boys up to London and give them a day out, which always included a good meal. It wasn't the best behaved boys he treated, but the boys who never received a food parcel or a visit.'

The routine and physical punishments including the strap were still in use, but there was less resentment among the boys. They recognised in Mr George, a man who meant what he said. They knew that if they behaved themselves, he would be aware of it, but equally if a boy kept breaking the rules, his name would be entered in his little black book and the usual punishments would follow.

The Superintendent was made up to General Superintendent and became responsible for all three Fegan's Homes. Yardley Gobion in Northants was a Home for small boys, Stony Stratford in Northants housed the majority of the schoolboys and boys over the age of fourteen were sent to the Training Farm at Goudhurst in Kent. They remained at the Farm until they reached the age of seventeen when they were given assistance in finding a job and accommodation in the outside world. One summer evening, when a number of the boys were playing a knock-about game of cricket, one or two of them stopped playing and ran across to that part of the field where it was possible to look up the garden path. The rest of the boys wondered what was up and followed. What they saw was a family of four walking down the path towards the sports field. One of the boys piped up, 'It's the new Superintendent and his wife and kids!'

'This chap should be all right,' said Ted Radcliffe, 'he's a family man!' The Homes hadn't had a change of Superintendent for more than twenty five years, so the rest of the staff and of course the boys wondered if the new man would institute any changes that would affect their daily routine.

Captain E.P. Flood had been a peace-time soldier with the Queen's Own Royal West Kent Regiment and was the Regimental Sergeant Major whilst serving in Malta during the Second World War. He rose to the rank of Captain and was taken prisoner of war by the Germans. He was awarded the Military Cross for action during a battle against the enemy in the Do Decanese on the Island of Leros.

One day, whilst being held in a prisoner of war camp, he was lining up for meal and roll-call parade when one of his fellow officers complained about the poor quality of the food. Capt. Flood pointed out to him that many poor boys back in England had food inferior to the food they were eating and were thankful for it.

Subsequently he gave a talk to the officers on the subject of needy boys in their own country. As a result, the officers present decided that should they survive the war, they would on returning to England open a Boys' Club to help such underprivileged boys. This was how the Brunswick Boys Club came into being after the war. Later, although having a full-time occupation as the Superintendent of Fegan's Stony Stratford, Capt. Flood still remained a firm supporter of the club.

Shortly after his arrival at Fegan's, the Deputy Superintendent said to him one day, 'Here, you'll be needing this sir,' handing the Captain a rolled up leather strap.

'What would I be doing with that?' enquired the Captain.

'Why, it's for punishing the boys when they step out of line sir,' he replied with some conviction.

'Please get rid of it,' said Capt. Flood. 'If I can't do this job without using a strap then I'm not fit for it!' He then made it clear to the staff that he wanted to change the way the Home was run. He wanted to have a good relationship with the staff and the boys. He intended to get to know the boys and to show them that life had a lot to offer them.

One memorable Monday morning, he stood on the Dining Hall platform and told the assembled boys:

'This Home for Fegan's Boys is not a prison. From this day on if any of you want to run away it will be easy. During the daytime the big iron front gates will remain open. You will be able to walk out through the gates instead of having to climb over the fence in the field. The large metal shutter that is always pulled down in the archway separating the parade ground from the front paths and gardens will be pulled down no more. I'm hoping though that before you think it necessary to run away you'll come to me first and let us work through together whatever is troubling you. We, the staff owe you that much.'

The boys were bowled over, gob-smacked. Nothing and no-one could have prevented what followed - a spontaneous outbreak of clapping that rose to a crescendo and didn't stop until Capt. Flood with a big grin on his face, put his hand up requesting them to stop.

A new day was dawning in the history of Fegan's Homes for Boys. Of course, most of the 'punishment' jobs still needed to be done by the boys in the Home, but after that day, all the jobs were fairly distributed and Spencer 50 was thrilled not to be able to find his number on the list of boys who had to scrub and polish the quarry tiles in the long passageway or the Dining Hall. He figured it was because 'the powers that be' knew he had already done more than his fair share. The School held in Stony Stratford was discontinued and Tony Spencer and Bob Bryant were among the first lot of boys to attend the local secondary school at the beginning of the school year 1946/1947. At first the Fegan boys were shunned by the other pupils and if there was anything wrong it would be blamed on the 'orphan' kids. But there was to be no turning back of the clock.

Whether the locals liked it or not, Fegan boys were about to become part of the community in which they lived.

Various clubs were introduced by the Captain and Tony Spencer, Bob Bryant and David Kent joined the Stamp Club and a lifelong interest in stamp collecting was sparked off at that time.

Tony also joined a woodwork class. Mr Mitchell, a master carpenter, taught the boys and under supervision Tony made a beautiful model of a yacht with layer upon layer of intricate fretwork. It stood about four feet high with a two foot mast. All that it needed was sails.

There was a kind plump lady in charge of the needle room called Miss Auger. She would tease all the boys incessantly about their socks. 'A stitch in time saves nine,' she would say when they gave her their socks full of holes to darn. One evening Tony went up to the needle room and knocked on the door. 'Come on in,' said a friendly voice. 'Oh its you Tony. What can I do for you young man?' said Miss Auger.

Tony proudly presented his finished model yacht.

'That's a grand looking boat. Did you make that all by yourself?' she asked.

'Yes, Miss Auger, but I badly need some sails for it and I was wondering if you sewing ladies, could possibly make some so that I'll be able to sail her when we go down to Lydd-on-Sea for summer camp?'

'Well young man and what'll you give us if we do make some sails for your boat?' she said having a bit of fun with him.

'Well, I haven't really got much money to pay for them,' he replied a trifle embarrassed by her question.

'Get along with you,' she laughed. 'We'll see what we can come up with!'

'Miss Auger made the most beautiful sails for my boat,' Tony recalls. 'It was made over the winter of 1947/48 and lost at sea in 1949. One day I took my boat, fully made up, painted and with sails and everything to launch it. I was as proud as Punch. But no-one had pointed out that I needed to attach a piece of string to it. I put the yacht into the water, not knowing the first thing about sailing. There was an off-shore breeze. It just keeled over onto the port tack and off it sailed, looking absolutely marvellous. Sadly I never laid eye on it again. I was devastated,' recalls Tony. 'I cried my eyes out like a baby. But that wasn't the end of my misfortune. On another occasion, I managed to do the same daft thing again with a model glider! Some people never learn!'

Another good thing Capt. Flood introduced to Fegan's was team work. Boys working together. To Tony's joy and delight, the first project he got the boys engaged in was making a hockey pitch in what used to be the old gardens.

Capt. Flood was a keen hockey player himself. He had played for the Army and loved the game. He measured out the gardens and it just so happened to be about the right size. Then he set the boys to work stripping off all the grass and plants and removing the stones. Then they worked in teams, turning over the earth with spades and finally raking it. It took about forty boys working hard for a week to get it ready. Tony hadn't been chosen to play in the cricket team or the football team, so he set his heart on being picked for the hockey team. He had learned to play ice hockey in Canada and had loved it, now he desperately wanted the opportunity to learn how to play hockey.

When they finished making the pitch, Capt. Flood selected two teams and Tony was thrilled to find that at last he had been picked. They were taught the rudiments of the game and it wasn't long before they were playing against each other. The time came when the Captain considered them good enough to represent Fegan's. Then they played against schools in Bucks, Bedford and all over. At last Tony was in his element. This was all part of the Superintendent's plan to integrate the Fegan boys into the sporting and social life of mainstream society and he made sure that they were good enough to compete and win.

The local folk who made up the congregation at Sunday services, were encouraged to befriend the boys and invite them home for tea at week-ends. Tony remembers with gratitude being invited out to the home of Mr and Mrs Clamp who lived in Newport Pagnall. Their son, Trevor attended the same school as Tony and was in his class. It was wonderful for him to be able to visit a small family home. They continued to keep in touch with him and took him along on family outings from time to time. His Aunts Gladys and Sylvia did visit their nephews occasionally and took them out for the day, but they never went to stay with either of them during the long school holidays. Tony went to a mixed school. The Fegan boys enjoyed getting to know the girls in the class. There were over one hundred and seventy boys in the Home at Stony so being in a class with 'girls' was a great novelty. The Fegan boys tried to get the girls to go out with them at the week-end on a Sunday afternoon for a walk, but the girls would turn up their noses and say, 'I'm not going out with the likes of you. You're a scruffy orphan. My parents wouldn't let me,' and that would be the end of it.

The boys learned that to be a Fegan boy, to be a boy from the Orphanage had a stigma attached to it. Some of the boys couldn't take the ragging and the unkind remarks so there would be a fight. They earned the reputation for being tough and rough. Tony reckoned it was better that than being regarded as snivelling weaklings.

Even though Tony could number Bob Bryant and David Kent among his pals he never got into scrapes with them. They were decent law-abiding boys. But he did get into scrapes with Charlie Jennings and Gerald Frost. They would sometimes take the long way home from school and hop over a wall or climb a fence, nip into an orchard and scrump some juicy apples or plums. On one occasion they were caught by an irate farmer who reported their misdemeanours to Capt. Flood. They were not punished with the strap or the cane, but they were not allowed to play hockey for a whole month. That really hit home.

But Spencer 50 still had a chip on his shoulder and was likely to fly off the handle if any boy called him names. Some of the boys would goad him and make fun of him, just to provoke an outburst. On more than one occasion his big brother would have to step in to stop them from bullying him.

Godfrey Spencer had been thirteen and a half when he was admitted to Fegan's. He had been in school for just six months when at fourteen his schooling ended. Like all the fourteen year old boys in Fegan's, he had been kept on at Stony Stratford to do jobs around the Home that the younger boys could not do. He worked in the boiler room, in the kitchen, in the bread room, became a house boy for the Floods and worked in the various gardens attached to the Home. He had managed to fit in at Fegan's and was popular with the staff and boys of his own age. He turned fifteen in December 1946 and on February 1947 he was transferred to the Training Farm at Goudhurst.

Tony felt very much alone after Godfrey left. He had mates, but he had always looked up to his older brother and almost without realising it had depended upon him for emotional and sometimes even physical support.

He became sullen and uncooperative and performed his duties in the Home under sufferance. When reprimanded by a member of Staff he became insolent. He deliberately broke rules that he considered stupid and punishment did nothing to change his attitude. In the staff room, Anthony Spencer became a frequent topic of conversation. His house master was given the challenging task of trying to sort him out.

Mr Coultas drew up a plan of action. He would corner the lad in the boiler room. No-one else would be likely to be around except the boy on duty and No.50 was that boy.

'I'd like a word with you Spencer,' he said.

'Yes sir,' said Tony sullenly.

'What is the matter with you Spencer?' enquired his house master. 'We know that your brother has left Stony and moved on to the Farm and you're feeling bad about it. But isn't it about time you stood on your own two feet! You're fourteen now. It won't be long before you'll be transferred to the Farm. Pull yourself together lad. Don't go down there with a record of bad behaviour. The staff at the Farm won't take kindly to you if they read in your report that you haven't pulled your weight here. Are you taking this in Spencer?'

'Yes sir,' replied Tony unconvincingly.

'That's all, you can get on with your work now.'

After Mr Coultas left Tony sat on the only stool in the boiler room. He wanted to think, to try and sort himself out. What was wrong with him? Why couldn't he be clever like his brother? Why couldn't he get on with things, and just fit in? He didn't know. He felt bad and miserable all the time now that his brother had gone to the Farm. Godfrey was the only 'family' he had. He didn't know how to 'pull himself together'. He was in a deep dark dungeon of a place and there was no way out. Now that his brother had gone to the Farm, he didn't know what to do about it. It seemed to him that he was in a deep dark dungeon and there was no way out.

Carey House - Fegans Homes

Fegan's staff

CHAPTER 12

Off with the old, on with the new

It was the week-end. Some of the boys had been kicking a ball about in the parade ground, but when it grew dark they went inside. They didn't fancy joining the boys playing draughts and chess.

'Let's go to the Mission Hall. They've got a meeting on there tonight,' said Dennis Brimstead.

'Not for me,' said Charlie Jennings, 'I get more than enough religion on Sundays, thank you very much!'

'How about you Tony?' said Dennis.

'Might as well,' replied Tony. 'I've got nothing else to do.'

The Saturday night meeting was open to folks from outside so there was always the chance of meeting up with some girls. There were refreshments at the end - lots of bread and butter, jam and cakes. The boys were always hungry and it beat going to bed with just some watery cocoa inside an empty stomach.

After Captain Flood became Superintendent, Mrs Flood took on the responsibility for the health and welfare of the boys until a suitably qualified nurse could be employed. Then Nurse Gillian Penn came to work at Stony Stratford. The boys took to her straight away. She had a great sense of fun and showed that she really cared about them.

She soon expressed an interest in helping to take services in the

Mission Hall together with her friend Methan. The three Sunday Services were very formal and attendance compulsory so she introduced a very informal service especially designed for young people on Saturday nights. She was able to arrange for visiting speakers who would appeal to young people such as London City Missioners and Youth for Christ leaders.

'Hello boys,' she said. 'I'm glad you could come. You choir boys will be able to help us out with the singing.'

They took their seats and noticed that the hall was filling up. They wondered who the speaker would be. Tony hoped whoever it was would be lively so that he wouldn't be tempted to nod off.

He needn't have worried. He enjoyed singing and the meeting got off to a really good start with a hymn he knew. But then something strange happened to him that he hadn't bargained for. He remembers standing up and singing the words:

'Give me a sight O Saviour of thy wondrous love to me. The love that brought thee down to earth to die on Calvary. O make me understand it. Help me to take it in. What it meant to thee, The Holy One, To bear away my sin.'

He'd sung those words before on other occasions, but they hadn't meant anything. It was just a hymn, but not this time. The words powerfully moved him as if they were coming out of his own broken heart. He found himself silently asking God, wherever he was, to help him. David Kent was sitting in front of him. He knew that David was sort of 'different' to the other lads. He made no secret of the fact that he was a Christian. His faith seemed to have the effect of making him a cheerful and hard-working lad, no matter how much the other boys taunted and goaded him. For the first time Tony wondered if he could ever be like that.

Two or three days later, he met up with Nurse Penn.

'All right, Tony?' she enquired?

'Well,' he said hesitatingly. 'I've got something on my mind and I can't seem to sort it out.'

'What would that be?' she asked.

'I don't really know, Miss,' he said. 'But it's something to do with the other night in the Mission Hall. I felt as if something was happening to make me different, but now I'm not so sure.'

Nurse Penn listened to his doubts and fears and was able to reassure him. In the weeks and months that followed, slowly the light began to dawn. The Bible became more relevant and a book he learned to treasure.

Tony says that in spite of many ups and downs in his life, he looks back to that time in Fegan's as the starting point for his future. He became a committed Christian due in part to the kindly interest and support given him by Nurse Penn when he was most in need of it. When the time came for him to be transferred to the Farm at Goudhurst, he was given a Report of Transfer to hand to the staff. He found the part of the report that detailed his progress since admission and was relieved and happy to read:

'This boy has progressed considerably in the last six months and as to his character and conduct - very honest and loyal, signed EP Flood.'

Bob Bryant and Tony Spencer had started at Fegan's in July 1945. Thereafter they became pals. It was probably due to the fact that they were the same age that they were transferred to Goudhurst together. They found it hard work, but a great improvement on the Stony Stratford Home. For a start, the food was better and there was more of it. A big consideration for growing lads.

The Training Farm at Goudhurst in Kent comprised 350 acres. About forty five boys between the ages of 14 - 18 were there at any one time, training to become farm workers. The daily routine depended very much on the time of year although the boys given the task of milking and looking after the cows could be engaged in that work all the year round.

The horse boys would be called up at 5.30 am. The horses on the farm were 6'3" Clydesdales, heavy duty horses used for ploughing. Later the lads were taught to drive tractors on the farm which replaced the horses and were used for ploughing, harrowing and seeding. Tony remembers there being a Fordson Major tractor and two Brownings on the farm at that time.

After breakfast at 8 am. the boys queued up in the farmyard and were delegated other jobs, depending on the time of the year. This could be thatching, making hay-ricks or beet clamping. Beet clamping, Tony learned entailed making a trench, lining it with straw, putting in the beet and then thatching it. 'It would keep like that all through the winter for animal fodder or as a vegetable for the boys to eat,' he said.

The boys were also taught hedging and ditching - making a ditch alongside the hedge. Tony reckons he could still make a good job of hedging even today.

But life down on the farm wasn't all work. There were some afternoons when the boys were given some time off. Then Tony, and his mate Bob Bryant, would walk to the town of Marden some five miles away. Once there they would make a bee-line for a favourite Pie Shop that sold hot steak and kidney pies. All the boys were given pocket money and they saved it to spend on outings such as these. Tony remembers paying out two old pennies for three delicious meat pies. Those were the days! On the whole it was a good life for the boys on the farm, but Tony couldn't settle. For some unknown reason a particular member of the staff kept finding fault with him and seemed to do all he could to make his life a misery. In the end he decided to write to his Aunt Gladys to ask her if he could visit with a view to discussing his future. He knew by then that he didn't want to make farming his life's work.

He was allowed to visit his Aunt for the Christmas Holidays for the first time since he'd been admitted to Fegan's. It was great being reunited with his older brother Godfrey who was living with his Aunt. He was now a man of the world and working hard for his living - or so he said!

'So, you don't want to do farm work then, Anthony?' said his Aunt impatiently. 'I'm sure I don't know what you'll be able to do then. You never got on well at your school work. Godfrey is doing marvellously well in Fegan's Head Office. But then, he was always such a bright boy.'

She sighed, 'Perhaps you should think of some sort of apprenticeship, Anthony. You need a career that will give you a good income and security!'

During the holiday, Tony travelled with his Aunt on the London underground. He would survey the other occupants in the carriage with great interest, wondering who they were and where they were going. This sort of outing was quite out of the ordinary for a Fegan's boy.

One day when they were travelling up to Baker Street to meet up with his brother with a view to doing some late Christmas shopping, a colourful advertisement caught his eye. **'JOIN THE NAVY AND SEE THE WORLD!'** It hit him like a bolt out of the blue. That's it, he thought. That's what I want to do!

He lost no time in conveying his new found ambition to his Aunt Gladys.

'So that's what you'd really like to do, is it Anthony?' she said doubtfully.

'Yes, Aunt Gladys' he said with enthusiasm. 'I've been on some big ships crossing the Atlantic and loved it. I was never sea-sick and we had some really rough weather on the outward journey to Canada.'

'Right then, Anthony,' said his Aunt Gladys. 'We shall see what we can do.'

When Tony returned to the Farm at Goudhurst, he felt hopeful that if anyone could help him get into the Navy that person would be his Aunt Gladys. He knew, now that she was convinced it was what he really wanted to do, she would move heaven and earth to get him in to the navy. And that's just what she did.

'Did you have a good Christmas Tony?' enquired Bob Bryant.

'Yeah, it was great,' said Tony. 'The food was the best part. Loads of hot roast dinners and Christmas pudding!'

'Some people have all the luck,' sighed Bob. 'I suppose that'll be the last you see of your Aunt until next Christmas eh?'

'Don't you be so sure,' said Tony mysteriously.

'What's up then, Tony?'

'You'll have to wait and see, won't you,' he replied. His eyes all lit up like a Christmas tree.

But no amount of badgering from his pal would induce him to say another word.

At the end of January 1950, just when Tony's faith in his Aunt Gladys was beginning to waiver, a letter arrived in the office at the farm from that same lady requesting that her nephew, Anthony Spencer, be allowed up to London for an interview at the Recruiting Office of the Royal Navy. Now the cat was really out of the bag! He was very nervous about the impending interview. It was by no means certain that he would get in. 'So you're off to join the navy, then? You could have told me. I thought I was one of your best mates!' said Bob Bryant sorry to be losing his friend.

'Well, I didn't tell you because there's always the chance that I won't get in. I may fail the medical or something. I wanted to wait until I was certain, that's all,' said Tony. The staff at the farm were excited for him and so wanted him to do well at the interview.

'We'll be thinking of you Spencer,' they said. 'Do your best.'

He went to his Aunt's house first. She spruced him up and got him to the appointment in good time.

'A big man in uniform with his chest covered with medals stood before me,' said Tony.

'So you want to join the Royal Navy, do you lad?' he bellowed.

'Yes sir,' replied Tony.

Tony didn't know it, but he was one of about a hundred young lads who had come to the Recruiting Office that day hoping to join the Navy. When he saw how many would-be young recruits were there, his heart sank. Surely they wouldn't all get in.

First they all had to sit a maths test and then an English test and then an aptitude test. Then their papers were collected and they were told to wait for further instructions. None of the boys said much. Tony drifted over to a tall window and looked out. It was raining.

After what seemed like an age, a naval officer came into the room and called out the names of four boys. Tony was one of them. The officer told them to follow him to the other end of the room.

'Right. I want you to write down the Lord's Prayer', he said.

The four lads looked surprised at this and one or two very uncomfortable, but Tony was delighted.

'Now I want you to write down the alphabet backwards - from 'z' to 'a'. You've got just twenty seconds, beginning now. He actually timed this test with a stopwatch.

Finally, Tony and his Aunt Gladys were called in to be told officially that he had been accepted as a boy seaman.

'We've had a quick look at the tests,' said the Recruiting Officer. 'There were four boys who were just a bit brighter than the rest. Your nephew was one of them. Congratulations Spencer! he said and shook Tony's hand. The interview was over. 'It did me the world of good to hear the Recruiting Officer tell me in front of my Aunt that I was one of the brighter lads who had come for interview that day' said Tony. 'She could put that in her pipe and smoke it!' Tony left the Farm on February 18th, 1950 and joined the Royal Navy on March 3rd. His brother Godfrey joined the Royal Air Force to do his National Service at more or less the same time so the Aunts had to say a fond farewell to them both. A new and exciting life in the Royal Navy was opening up for sixteen year old boy seaman Spencer and he intended to do his utmost to make his Aunts, and all the staff and lads at Fegan's, proud of him.

CHAPTER 13

Raw Recruits

March 1st 1950 dawned, a day to remember in Anthony Spencer's calendar. He was off to join the Royal Navy. 'Don't forget to write!' said Aunt Sylvia. 'Send a letter straight away to let us know you've arrived safely,' said Aunt Gladys, not to be outdone in her bid to receive news from her nephew before her sister. After all, she had moved heaven and earth to get him into the Navy.

'Of course, I'll write, but don't you worry Aunts,' said the cheerful soon-to-be sailor, 'I'll be all right!' Then he boarded the train, leant out of the window and grinning from ear to ear, waved an energetic 'goodbye'. As the train pulled out of Liverpool Street station. They could still see his unruly red-hair long after his waving hand was out of sight.

They sighed. They had said their 'goodbyes' to both of their nephews on the same day. Godfrey had gone to do his national service in the Royal Air Force and now Anthony left to join the navy. They were not displeased with the way things had turned out for their nephews. Things could have been worse, much worse.

There seemed to Tony to be a lot of lads on the train and he wondered if any of them were going to Ipswich. He paced up and down the corridor too excited to sit still. He bumped into one of the boys.

'Where you off to then?' he asked.

'I'm off to Ipswich.'

'That's funny,' said Tony. 'So am I. You wouldn't be joining the Navy would you?'

'Yes. I think half the train is filled up with recruits,' laughed the lad. 'My name's Derek Miles, what's yours?'

'Tony Spencer,' said Tony and they shook hands enthusiastically.

'Look here, why don't you get your things and join us?' said Tony's new-found mate. 'I don't mind if I do,' said Tony.

The journey didn't seem so long and tedious after that. The lads, who were bound for *HMS Ganges* told each other jokes, played cards and were up and down like a Jack-in-a-box, but suddenly it was 'action stations'- a quick bit of smartening up and they all tumbled out onto the platform at Ipswich.

A Very Important Person, looking as smart as sixpence marched up to the waiting recruits. 'Follow me,' bellowed the chief petty officer and they were all bundled into a waiting lorry. In no time at all they arrived at the new entry annexe attached to *HMS Ganges*. The lads, all aged between sixteen and seventeen were as high as a kite, full of excitement and apprehension. A new life of adventure was about to open up before them and they relished the prospect of joining the world's best Navy to see the world.

They fell out of the lorry and then there was an uproar of laughter as the chief petty officer gave the order for them to 'fall in'. They were a motley crew, with long hair, an assortment of civvy clothes that gave no hint of the career they had chosen. 'Right! Quick march into the Mess Deck. Find yourself a bed and stand in front of it,' was the order of the day.

The Mess Deck turned out to be a long hut with beds down either side with a businesslike dining area at one end. On each bed was a rolled up mattress and a pillow. Tony Spencer, Derek Miles and Peter Triggs who had got to know each other on the journey made a bee-line for the beds nearest to the dining area thinking of grub and hoping there would be some in the near future. It was good thinking. A couple of seamen brought in a dixie full of piping hot tea and a trolley piled high with sandwiches.

'Right lads, fifteen minutes for refreshments.' The lads still stood standing to attention beside their beds. 'Well, get on with it!' yelled the petty officer' and then there was a stampede for grub. Some of the lads were still queuing for their tea and sandwiches when the time allotted for refreshments ran out.

'Right lads. Find your beds and stand to attention at the end of it!' was the order.

'Anthony Spencer?'

'Yes, sir,' said Tony.

'Your number will be PJX 889495. Remember it. It'll by your number throughout your naval career.

'Yes sir,' said Tony. 'Thank you, sir.'

The following day reveille was at 6.00 a.m. Some of the boys groaned and rolled over ready to go back to sleep. It seemed like the middle of the night to them. It was a bitterly cold March morning. But young Tony Spencer had already lived through many such mornings down at the Stony Stratford orphanage. He nipped out of bed smartly knowing that being first in the wash room meant you would be dressed and ready for breakfast first. He had always had a healthy appetite.

Well set up for the day, they were kitted out and introduced to the uniform they as boy seamen were soon to have the honour of wearing. Along with trousers and two white fronts, they were each given a black silk.

The chief petty officer demonstrated how to dress correctly in the uniform. He held up the black silk. 'Can any of you tell me what the black silk is worn for?' he asked. Every boy seemed at a loss. 'You've all heard of Admiral, Lord Nelson?'

'Yes sir,' replied the boys in unison.

'We wear this black silk in his memory. It commemorates the

Battle of Trafalgar on 21st October 1805 when the great man died.'

On the fourth day, the chief petty officer told the lads to get themselves and their kit ready for inspection by the Divisional Officer. This was followed by frantic efforts to get everything ship-shape. Then Lt. Commander Gillespie entered the Mess to say a few words to each lad. He stopped at Tony Spencer's bed. 'Anthony Spencer?'

'Yes sir,' said Tony.

'Where are you from Spencer?'

'I come from Mr Fegan's Home for Boys which is an Orphanage in Stony Stratford North Bucks, sir,' he replied.

'Fine, Spencer. I've had many of your boys through here. I'ts good to have you with us,' and off he went until he'd finished the inspection with, 'carry on'.

One of the boys, a very tall boy who was over six feet announced to the rest of the Mess,

'Hey boys, you'll be interested to learn that we've got a little workhouse brat here with us. What do you think of that?' followed by raucous laughter from him and the rest of the Mess. Tony, who measuring all of five feet two inches, made up for in courage what he lacked in inches, was incensed. He wasn't going to stand for that. Up he jumped onto one of the beds, and then he leaped over a couple more until he was near enough to land the unsuspecting scoffer a swinging blow on his unsuspecting jaw. The tall lad was instantly felled as if he were a large standing tree earmarked for timber. He landed with a thud on the Mess deck and had to be transported from there to Sick Bay. The Mess was stunned. It had all happened in a flash. Anthony Spencer was immediately put on a charge and brought before the Divisional Officer.

'We don't really countenance this sort of behaviour, Spencer,' he said, 'but taking into account the provocation in this case, I will overlook it. Case dismissed, but watch your step, Spencer!'

That was the one and only time Anthony Spencer RN was ever on a charge. The other lad was out of action for all of three weeks. Later on, when they got to know each other better they actually became good mates! Every move he made in the Navy after that he never got bullied. Somehow or other his reputation for being able to stand up for himself always went ahead of him.

In the days that followed the new recruits were put through their paces to determine which path their naval career was to follow. After undergoing many and varied aptitude tests, eight lads were selected for communications training - four for visual communications and four for wireless telegraphy. Tony and his mates Derek Miles and Peter Triggs together with five other boy seamen were then transferred to the Communications Section in the main part of *Ganges*. They were put into Greyhound Mess and were taught flags together with international and military Morse code using both lights and flags. Unfortunately after playing just one good game of rugby, Tony landed up in hospital, not with injuries sustained on the playing field, but with an unexpected fever - scarlet fever. This was a stroke of bad luck, but his tutor, Yeoman Sutton made sure that he didn't lose out. He got his mates to send him semaphore messages from the water tower, which he received and noted down, helped considerably by a very pretty nurse who had taken him under her wing. In this way he was able to keep up to scratch with learning the Morse code by flags and flashing lights.

Yeoman Sutton got everyone of his lads through the course successfully and they all went on to become good signalmen and a credit to him.

The new recruits enjoyed their time in *Ganges*. They had to learn to touch-type, were taught the thrills and spills of sailing and Tony learned to cox a twenty seven foot open boat called a whaler. Cross-country running was Tony's sport and hockey. He left *Ganges* in March 1951 having been in training there for just over a year. He'd gained in confidence and skills and was ready for his first draft to HMS *Dolphin* for submarine training.

He was attached to HMS *Affray* where he spent the following six weeks sea training, diving, being put through the tank and survival training. He enjoyed it enormously. They were a good bunch of men and they taught him a lot. Then he was sent on retard leave and went to spend it with his Aunt Sylvia at 141 Como Road, Forest Hill.

It was April 15th, 1951. Tony was in the bath. He can remember it as if it were yesterday.

'It came over the radio - '*SUBSMASH* HMS *Affray!*' My aunt came up the stairs and shouted - 'Your boat, Anthony. It's gone down! There's been an accident. The boat you've been on. It's sunk!'

'It was a terrible shock,' said Tony. 'Seventy five men had died. I knew some of them. I had worked with them, ate with them, slept with them for six weeks. I was just seventeen. It was a terrible blow!'

Years later, when a friend came over from Canada and Tony took him to look over HMS *Alliance.* a sister ship to the *Affray*, as he went down into the sub, it all came flooding back to him. 'I could see those men who had died sitting at the controls,' he said. 'I couldn't take it. I had to get off the sub.

When Tony went back off leave, it seemed that everybody had been affected by the tragic loss of HMS *Affray.* It made it easier for him to know that he wasn't the only seaman who had been devastated by the news.

The powers-that-be decided that Anthony Spencer was too young for submarines. His ship and ship-mates had gone down, he was therefore drafted to a sea-going battle class destroyer in general service, HMS *Cadiz* in Portsmouth Harbour. It was a member of the Home Fleet. Tony would be in the company of yeomen who knew what he had been through. They would keep him busy and look out for him. He had taken a big blow at a young age, but the naval officers who had been responsible for his visual communications training thus far, had every confidence that he would survive and move on. They were to be proved right.

Boatwork - HMS Ganges Tony_end_ right

CHAPTER 14

Signal boy's first ship

Seventeen year old signal boy, Tony Spencer was excited and apprehensive when he walked up the gangplank to join his first ship. This was it. This was the real thing. Now he would have a chance to put into practise all that he had had drummed into him at HMS *Ganges* about flags and semaphore and light signals, until he was eating, sleeping and dreaming the stuff.

HMS *Cadiz* was a battle class destroyer, 2315 tons, 335ft x 40ft fitted with twin 4.5 guns, 4 x 2 40mm Oerlikon guns and 2 x 4 torpedo tubes. It was built by Fairfield in Glasgow in 1944, but not commissioned until September 17th 1946. The ship's pennant was D79. The ship's company comprised twenty officers and 310 men.

Anthony Gerald Spencer became 'boy first class' on 21st September 1950 and a signal boy, on 13th May 1951 his first day on *Cadiz.*

'I'm signalman Bill Dunstan,' said the much bigger confident looking sailor who welcomed him on board. He had done his apprenticeship as a war-time signalman, but was still only twenty-four. 'Tony Spencer, isn't it? I'll show you to the Mess Deck.'

Tony was relieved to be able to follow close on the heels of his new mentor who soon let him know that he wasn't the only new crew arriving that day. He was one of twenty. They were not all in communications. 'I think you'll know Derek Miles. He was with you in *Ganges* ,' he said.

'Yes, I know him all right,' said Tony.

'He hasn't come aboard yet. Leave your kit here and I'll show you around the ship. She's a beaut. We've got a great bunch of men on board. The officers aren't all bad either,' he said with a wry grin. 'The Commanding Officer, J.F.D. Bush, is top brass. A war vet, decorated for valour and all that sort of thing.' He was shown the Flag Deck and the lockers on either side where the flags he would be using were stored. The Flag Deck was situated just below the bridge. Visual communications were also transmitted from there.

The ship was a hive of industry and order. While he was being shown around, he could see flags being hoisted and semaphore messages being sent out, then he noticed a young signalman in the main signal office sitting at a typewriter recording each signal as it came in. A yeoman was standing at the ready to take it up to the Chief Yeoman on bridge. Tony wondered if he'd ever be as quick and efficient as the young men he'd been observing. He seriously doubted it. Bill Dunstan seemed to read his mind. 'Putting the wind up you is it mate?' he said. 'Of course it is. Don't worry. You'll soon get the hang of it.'

'By the way, you'll have to sign this,' he said placing before Tony a copy of the Official Secrets Act. 'It's just routine. Everybody in communications has to sign it. A lot of what comes in or goes out is run-of- the-mill, but occasionally it's top secret or highly confidential. We're not allowed to talk about our work to any of the ship's company, o.k? Good!'

He was taken to the electrical branch who were responsible for all the electrics on board the ship including repairs to equipment and maintenance of the powerful signal lamps that the visual signals branch used. Tony would get to know these chaps well.

'You need to know your way around because you'll be delivering messages all over the ship. Don't forget to wait for a signature from the officer in charge or you'll be in big trouble,' said Bill.

He knew that being part of visual signals branch meant that

Tony would have very little to do with the seamen on board and nothing to do with the stokers. He wanted to impress upon the new boy that everybody on board *Cadiz* had an equally important role to play to ensure the efficient running of the ship.

The seamen are normally responsible for the ropes, wires and cables,' said his mentor. 'They man the guns. They see to the anchoring and provisioning of the ship and generally keep her in good order.'

Then they went below and Bill introduced Tony to some of the stokers who were responsible for the oil-fired diesel engines. The older man had a laugh and a joke with them. 'They are all good men,' he said appreciatively, 'remember we'd be lost without them!'

'You didn't know that we have Writers on board ship, did you?' Bill said. 'They are very important people. They handle our pay and order all the ships stores.'

'If you are sick at any time, you'll need to report to the Medical Officer. Destroyers carry a doctor, but if surgery is required you may have to be transferred to another ship that has better facilities on board. But we don't expect a healthy young whippersnapper like you ever to need the services of the medics, do we?' Bill chuckled and gave the young signal boy a hearty slap on the back that nearly sent him reeling.

By the end of the tour, Tony's head was aching from information overload. Later when he met up with other new crew members in the mess, he was quite relieved to find that they were all feeling apprehensive and doubtful if they would ever measure up to all that was required of them. All, that is, except signal boy Derek Miles.

'Hello there Tony,' he said when he met up with his old mate from *Ganges*.

'Have they shown you around?' enquired Tony. 'It's an enormous ship. There's so much going on. The Flag Deck people are amazing - so fast. I can't imagine ever being that good!'

'Sure you will,' said Miles. 'They'll lick us into shape in no time at all!'

Tony sighed. It was obvious that Miles hadn't changed a bit. He always was a cocky little devil.

The main purpose of destroyers as part of the Home Fleet was to visit different countries showing the flag - a goodwill mission. Their other duties involved Fleet manoeuvres. *Cadiz* had twenty new crew on board so that meant the whole of the ship's company had to do a 'work-up' until everyone on board knew their jobs inside and out. Fleet manoeuvres were designed with this particular purpose in mind.

Tony learned fast by having to turn his hand to anything and everything - 'Take this message to electrics and be quick about it!' 'Go down to the galley and get us four mugs of tea, pronto!' 'Get these flags out and get them up, now! 'C'mon, move it lad. Don't hang about!' and so on. He was at everyone's beck and call, but he loved it. He was always on the move, outside in all weathers, in his element, a born sailor.

The *Cadiz* was put on 'chasing duty', practising with the fleet. She was ordered to chase the aircraft carrier HMS *Indefatigable*. It was Tony's job to send the signal to the ships following behind by flags and semaphore when they were about to turn into the wind and increase their speed. Then *Indefatigable* would immediately start 'flying off'.

The North Sea was rough at the best of times making it difficult for the small two-seater aircraft to take off, but eventually they would manage to get airborne. They would fly around and then land back on the flight deck practising 'bumps'. And bump those sea-furies did, up and down, down and up. A wire hook attached to a cable which came down underneath the aircraft was the only means of preventing them from overshooting the flight deck.

The pilots had to take their planes up again and again. Tony and his mates would watch them mesmerised. Then one day disaster struck. One of the sea-furies overshot the flight deck and crashed like a crazy kite into the turbulent sea.

'I saw the pilot get out in double quick time, but the observer was struggling and then the plane sank,' said Tony. 'I couldn't believe my eyes. It was terrible. There was nothing anyone could do.' He came to dread these 'flying off' exercises. 'Every so often it would happen again. A plane would overshoot the runway and plunge into the sea. Another plucky pilot or his observer would inevitably be unable to escape before the aircraft sank. We signalmen would hold our breath and pray that they would make it back safely and were always cut up when they didn't.

Manoeuvres over, the Fleet sailed for Scandinavia. It broke up and the ships dispersed to show the flag in different ports. HMS *Cadiz* went to Sweden. Tony was on the Flag Deck as they negotiated the fjords and islands until they entered the waterway bringing the ship right into the centre of the beautiful city of Stockholm. As a young lad of seventeen, he was all eyes and ears, hungry for the sights and sounds of new places and new people. The crew knew the drill. They had to fulfil their shipboard duties and then all spruced up were allowed day shore leave to meet and mingle with the friendly natives.

Tony Spencer, Derek Miles, Bill Dunstan and one of his mates explored Stockholm together. They were in high spirits and it wasn't long before they found an attractive café and ordered drinks. In spite of causing a stir among the young Swedish clientèle, they couldn't make much headway due to their inability to converse in the local lingo.

Tony was flabbergasted when the waiter brought four tankers as big as buckets to their table filled with lager. 'Steady on,' he said to the waiter, 'I ordered Coca Cola. You can take one of these back!'

'Take it back?' said Bill with a look of disgust on his face, 'don't be so stupid! Leave it here. I'll have it, no problem!'

They knew that young Spencer was a teetotaller. They could live with that, but they were persuaded that he didn't know what he was missing. They then proceeded to drink themselves legless. Young Spencer was the only signalman who managed to get back on board that night none the worse for his first outing to a foreign city.

An unexpected treat was to follow. Three of the youngest members of the crew, including Tony Spencer and Derek Miles had been invited to stay for a week as a guest of a Swedish family. 'Just what the doctor ordered,' said Derek Miles cheerfully.

'Some people have all the luck,' said Bill Dunstan. 'Don't forget to let those beautiful blonde girls know that you've got two lonely mates on board who'd love to make their acquaintance!'

'You've got a hope!' said Derek Miles wryly.

Tony was driven out by his host to the mountains and was very happy to be introduced to his three beautiful daughters.

The youngest was called Ingrid. She had just turned seventeen. He had high hopes! But it soon became apparent that not knowing even a smattering of Swedish was a definite drawback. Another disincentive was black sausage, black bread and pickled herring - not exactly what a young and forever hungry boy sailor expected for breakfast. He badly missed fried eggs, bacon and fried bread. The Swedes he found ate a lot of uncooked, cold food so there was never meat and two veg. on the menu for supper when he was ravenous. At the end of the day, he wasn't too upset to learn that not only Ingrid, but her two gorgeous sisters had big, handsome and considerably older Swedish boyfriends!

The whole of the ship's company were subsequently invited to various functions and taken on sight-seeing tours. Derek Miles and Bill Dunstan loved Swedish girls, Swedish lager and soon warmed to the Swedish way of life and only reluctantly tore themselves away, promising faithfully to return, when it was time for their ship to sail for other ports.

HMS *Cadiz* joined up once again with the fleet in the North Sea to undertake further manoeuvres which took them into Mirmansk. This time Tony was put on watch-keeping for the first time. It was a first dog-watch from 4 o'clock to 6 o'clock with Bill Dunstan who said he did all right.

Then it was back on the Scandinavian run calling in at Copenhagen. This time Tony went off exploring on his own. He wandered around the shops and was on his way to see the famous mermaid in the Tivoli Gardens when he saw a couple of British sailors walking towards him. 'One of them was an old Fegan boy,' said Tony. 'We hadn't been in contact for three years or more.'

'Hello Roy!' said Tony

'Why if it isn't Spencer 50. How are you mate and how's that brother of yours?' said Roy Sheldrake.

'What are you doing in Copenhagen?' asked Tony.

'We're with the aircraft carrier *Indomitable*. She's a terrific ship. We're aircraft fitters!' said Roy proudly. 'What ship are you on?'

'HMS *Cadiz,* a battle-class destroyer. I'm in visual signals. She's a great ship,' said Tony loyally. They nodded approvingly.

'You doing anything?'

'Not really, but I've got to be back on board by 9.00 pm.'

'That's all right. We've got a bit of shopping to do, then it's back to the ship. Would you like to come on board and have a look round?'

'Not half!' said Tony. They did some sight-seeing and managed to buy a few presents for family and friends back home and then it was time for Tony to have his first look over an aircraft carrier. Roy took great pleasure in showing him around. He was a couple of years older than Tony and wanted to impress him with his vastly superior knowledge and experience. He succeeded. Tony was gob-smacked!

'It was a huge ship,' said Tony, 'Absolutely amazing!' He wandered around enthralled. He told Roy about the manoeuvres his ship had been on and chasing the aircraft carrier *Indefatigable.* 'Those pilots had guts,' he said. 'They take their life in their hands every time they fly off!'

Then Roy introduced him to a pilot who flew barracudas and sea-furies. He was a bit embarrassed by Tony's obvious admiration. 'Look here old chap,' he said, 'There's nothing to it. It's what we do - our job. That's all!' and he sauntered off.

'Well, I think their terrifically brave, anyway,' said Tony. Roy couldn't help but agree.

He never did get to see the Flag Deck, but it didn't matter. It had been a marvellous day.

'Remember me to Godfrey when you write and give him my best,' said Roy when it was time for him to leave *Indomitable*.

Cadiz left Scandinavia and set sail for Portsmouth. They arrived in August and Tony was given some shore leave. He was bigger, heavier, stronger and he'd changed in other ways too. He was no longer apologetic. He was confident, a good signalman affirmed by his peers. He couldn't wait to see if his Aunts would notice the difference.

First ship - HMS Cadiz 1951

CHAPTER 15

All the nice girls love a sailor

After the first happy reunion was over, Aunt Sylvia's hospitality left much to be desired. Tony couldn't find anywhere to put his feet up and relax. Sylvia Butler was still the busy district midwife who regularly held antenatal and postnatal clinics in her house and in Tony's bedroom. He found it very embarrassing passing these ladies on the stairs and it happened four or five times a week.

'I'm going down to Stony Stratford to see the boys,' he said one morning to his aunt, thinking that he might also meet a nice girl or something like that.

'Well, perhaps it's just as well,' she said. 'I've a lot of ladies booked in for the next week or two, so I'm afraid I'll be needing your room!'

'I'll pop round to see Aunt Gladys before I go,' he said, knowing full well that if he didn't she would be offended.

By the time he was ready to leave the house, there was the sound of lively chatter and giggles coming from the hallway. Sylvia Butler's ladies-in-waiting were gathering for their appointments. Tony sighed. There was no way he could avoid them. 'Excuse me,' he said, again and again as he brushed passed his aunt's clients on the stairs. He was even more embarrassed when they touched his collar for 'luck'. But his face reddened when one of the young women started the others off singing: 'All the nice girls love a sailor. All the nice girls love a tar. For there's something about a sailor - And you know what sailors are!'

'Stop it Carrie, you're making the young man blush,' said a pretty plump mum-to-be. They all laughed. He could see the funny side of it, but his aunt's house was definitely no place for a bright-eyed and bushy-tailed young naval signalman. He beat a hasty retreat.

When he turned up at Fegan's in Stony Stratford, he met up with Captain Flood, the superintendent.

'Tony,' he said, 'how nice to see you! What are you doing down here?'

'I've got a spot of leave so I thought I'd come down and stay for a few days,' he said.

'Well, you won't last a few days here. We're all going off to camp,' said the captain.

'I should like to tag along, but I haven't brought the right sort of gear with me,' said Tony doubtfully.

'Why don't you come anyway,' said the Captain. A couple of the house masters are off sick. We could really do with your help!'

That settled it. He rang his aunt and asked her to meet him on Waterloo Station with the clothes that he needed to go on a camp. So that is what happened. She also put into his hand a very welcome ten shilling note - which was a lot of money in those days.

'Have a good time, Anthony,' she said, feeling a bit guilty about having to constantly turf him out of his room whenever he came home on leave.

When he eventually found the camp site in Poole, he was surprised to find a dozen shabby looking bell tents down one side of the field and about the same number of fancy-looking tents down the other. In the middle was a large marquee which looked as if it was intended to be used by both lots of campers.

He was noisily welcomed by all the Fegan boys who looked upon him as a bit of a hero. 'It's great you could come Tony ' they said. 'What's going on here boys? enquired Tony, pointing to the 'fancy' tents.

'It's girls!' said a disgusted ten-year old Fegan boy. 'They're from a place called Gloucester. The Life Brigade or something. Why did they have to come on our camp site and spoil everything!'

Tony grinned. He didn't share Bob Martin's prejudice against the opposite sex. In fact he was rather looking forward to meeting some of them.

Being in the navy cooped up with a lot of blokes was all right, they were good mates, but he was looking for another sort of mate. He wanted to find a special sort of girl who wouldn't fool around while he was away at sea. He didn't know why, but he had a gut feeling that he was due to meet her in this place.

That night he shared a tent with some of the senior boys who bombarded him with questions about the navy, where he'd been, what he'd been up to.

'Would you recommend it as a career?' asked a short freckle-faced kid wearing specs.

'Yeah, it's a good life if you love the sea in all of her moods. On board your ship mates are important. You learn to look out for each other, to lean on each other.' Early the next morning everybody had chores to do and Tony was kept very busy making himself generally useful. There were over a hundred and fifty boys at the camp to be kept out of mischief. Everything was running smoothly when out of the corner of his eye he noticed a couple of lovely young girls, about his own age hovering around the big marquee.

'Hi there,' he said. 'Are you with the Girls' Life Brigade?' 'Yes,' said a pretty girl with short fair hair and cornflower blue eyes. He was all but bowled over.

'My name is June' she said. 'Oh and this is my friend Nita.'

'Tony Spencer,' he said. 'I was a Fegan boy, until I left to join the navy.'

'Oh yes,' June said. 'We saw you arrive in your uniform. We thought you looked smashing, didn't we Nita?'

'Yes,' said Nita with a quiet shy smile.

'Well, it's been nice meeting you, but I'll have to get on,' said Tony, 'we're bound to meet up again. See yer.'

'Oh yes, I do hope so!' said June gushingly. 'I just love boys in uniform, especially sailors.'

Later when he had half a minute to himself, Tony thought about the girls. He was flattered in a way by the one calling herself, 'June'. She'd made a real play for him. But he couldn't really see her as the 'waiting kind'. She'd be good for a giggle now, but he was after more than that. He wondered about her friend, Nita? She didn't have much to say for herself, but her shyness appealed to him. He decided that if he got the chance, he'd ask her out.

He shrugged his shoulders and gathered the boys together who were on washing-up duty. 'Come on lads there are some lovely pots and pans just waiting for you to give them a good scrub!' 'Oh no,' they groaned. 'If you're thinking of joining the navy, you'll be expected to jump to it, whatever job you're given. No shirkers allowed in Her Majesty's Senior Service! Let's get stuck in, then we'll have a game of football!'

That was more like it.

A couple of days later, Tony was given some time off. He thought he'd take the bus into Bournemouth. Who should be standing at the bus stop, but the two pretty girls he had already had the pleasure of meeting.

'Oh,' said June, going all soppy and silly 'fancy meeting you again. Where are you off to all on your own?'

'I thought I'd take a look around Bournemouth.'

'That's where we're going,' said June. He turned to speak to her friend. 'I wonder if you wouldn't mind showing me around when we get there, Nita, isn't it?'

Nita blushed and smiled at Tony. He noticed the dimples in her cheeks, her long dark hair bouncing up and down upon her shoulders and most of all her beautiful grey-green eyes. She was a little cracker!

When the bus came, they went upstairs and Tony made sure that he sat next to her. Her flighty friend was puzzled. What could a sailor see in Nita! She knew her friend, he wouldn't get very far with her, she could guarantee it!

Tony and Nita seem to hit it off right away. Tony dared to take hold of her hand and he was thrilled that she didn't seem to mind.

By the end of the holiday, Tony knew that he'd found the girl of his dreams, but he wasn't sure that she felt the same way about him.

'Nita,' he said on their last evening together as they sat holding hands and staring into the camp fire. 'I'm sure I was meant to come to camp just to meet you!'

'Yes, it's been a great camp this year. Our girls have really had a happy time!'

'But what about you Nita, have you had a happy time?'

'Of course,' she said. She knew what he was getting at, but she had reservations. She had only recently been hurt by the break up with her steady boy friend. She didn't want to get her heart broken again. She was fond of Tony. He was a lot of fun to be with, but she hadn't known him very long.

'I thought you were beginning to care for me Nita, as I care for you? but perhaps I was wrong?'

Nita didn't say anything. Tony couldn't possibly have guessed her thoughts. He took her silence to mean that he didn't stand a chance with her.

'What a fool, I've been,' he said flatly. 'I was going to ask you to be my girl, to write to me, to wait for me. I know we haven't known each other for very long, but I care for you Nita and I don't want anyone else.'

Nita was surprised at the depth of his feelings. Their friendship had meant more to him than she had dared to hope. She had so enjoyed his company and knew that when he went away, she'd miss him very much.

'Tony, I do care about you and I'd love to write you,' she said.

'Oh, Nita,' he said, as he drew her close to him and kissed her. She found herself able to respond and trust that her sailor boy would not let her down. Signalman Anthony Spencer went back on board HMS *Cadiz* as happy as a sandboy. He had found himself a wonderful girl and even his ship mates could see the stars in his eyes!'

'Our Tony's found himself a girl!' Bill Dunstan announced to the Mess. 'Yahoo! yahoo!' they shouted, they cheered and banged their mess tins on the table and stamped their feet to show that they heartily approved.

The *Cadiz* sailed down to Portugal. Nita kept her word and wrote to Tony. He loved her letters and read them over again and again. They continued their courting in this way and their feelings for each other grew and developed until they became committed to the relationship.

He wrote to his aunts in London, informing them that he had met the most wonderful girl in the world on his recent holiday in Poole and asking if he could bring her up to London to meet them on his next leave.

Tony's news was not well received by his aunts.

'What does he have to go and get himself mixed up with this girl for!' said Sylvia Butler crossly. 'He's only just met her, so he can't possibly know anything about her!' 'Well, we'll have to wait and see, won't we,' said her friend and companion, Emily. 'No good jumping to conclusions about her Sylvia until we've found out what she's like!' Emily was always willing to give people the benefit of the doubt.

'You're just annoyed that he hasn't got himself attached to one of those twin girls you're always on about that go to your church,' said Gladys.

'They are perfectly respectable girls,' said Sylvia, 'and he could do a lot worse. It's not too late. He's very young. He may yet change his mind!'

'I don't think so,' said Gladys. 'According to his last letter, he's bringing her up to London to meet us the first week-end in October. That's in a couple of weeks time!'

'I'm going to write and put him off,' said Sylvia firmly. 'It won't be convenient having her to stay with us!'

'Don't you dare,' said Gladys. 'She can stay over at my place and Anthony can stay here with you in his old room. I'm dying with curiosity to see what this girl is like that our Tony appears to have fallen head-over-heels in love with!'

'You do talk such rot, Gladys,' said Sylvia. 'What would you know about young love! It's a fleeting, fickle emotion and not to be taken seriously.'

Her sister's remarks wounded Gladys. She had once been in love with a young soldier. They had planned to spend the rest of their lives together, but he had been killed just before the end of the first World Ward. She was only twenty four, but it broke her heart. She'd never got over it and her sister knew it. Sometimes she hated her sister.

Needless to say it was with some fear and trepidation that Nita Barton travelled up to London with Tony to meet his spinster aunts. He had written a lot about them in his letters. It was obvious that he felt he owed them so much for looking after him and his brother. She knew it mattered to Tony what they thought and was anxious to make a good impression for his sake. 'This is Nita,' said Tony proudly introducing his girl friend to his Aunt Gladys.

'Hello, Nita,' she said, shaking her hand warmly. 'I've heard so much about you from Anthony. I feel I know you already!

'How do you do?' said Sylvia Butler formally. Nita felt awkward and embarrassed. They had tea and scones and made small talk, but Nita couldn't relax. She knew she was being given a critical appraisal by Tony's aunts. In particular she sensed Sylvia Butler's hostility and she feared that she would use her considerable influence over her nephew to break up their relationship.

As soon as she could Tony's Aunt Sylvia managed to get her

nephew on his own. She waded in right away with her objections. 'I can't understand you Anthony,' she said irritably, 'taking up with a simple country girl like that. She can hardly string more than two words together!'

'I don't know what you mean, Aunt,' said Tony, determined that whatever his Aunt Sylvia said wasn't going to change a thing.

'I'm sure she's a nice girl, of course, but she's not the one for you Anthony. You are going up in the world and she won't be able to measure up to that high standard.'

You don't know Nita,' said Tony shaking his head. 'She's just the sort of girl I've been looking for and I'm jolly lucky to have found her.'

'But you don't know anything about her,' said his Aunt. Where does she come from? What does her father do for a living? Is he a professional man and what about her mother? Breeding is important, Anthony! Promise me you won't get serious with this girl at least until you've found out about her parents and what sort of people they are?'

'No, I can't make you any such promise, Aunt Sylvia,' said Tony. 'We'll just have to see how things work out, won't we?' And that was that as far as Tony Spencer was concerned.

Nita Barton

*Nita & Tony meeting each
other at Bournmouth*

Chapter 16

Nita Barton

The Bartons were from the West Country. Harry George Barton was a railway porter in the late 1800swhen he met and married Louisa Parsons. He had opportunities for advancement in the north of England so they moved up to Yorkshire where six of their eight children were subsequently born. Emily was born in 1899. She died in infancy. Henry Bruce known as 'Bruce' was born in 1900. He became Nita Barton's father.

When Bruce was eight years old, the Barton family moved again. Harry brought his growing family to live in Magdela Road on the outskirts of Gloucester. He was still working for the railways, but had other plans for his children.

Bruce and his brother Fred were apprenticed to a master carpenter and joiner. Charles became an engineer, but contracted tuberculosis and diabetes and spent years in and out of hospital. Harry's four daughters left school and went to work for the Gloucester Shirt Company. Only the youngest, Nora Eileen, was destined to marry.

Ambitious Harry moved for the last time to Barton Street. 'The Bartons of Barton Street.' It had a nice ring to it and this time Harry was able to buy the property.

When he was a young man and ready for 'courting', Bruce met a very attractive young lady - Verona Violet Bloodworth. She came from a large family of five boys and two girls. Verona was the youngest Bloodworth to arrive on the scene. When she was born, the story goes, that her big brother Sid, took one look at her and said, 'Look at that little dolly, Ma!' She was christened, 'Verona Violet Bloodworth,' but from then on was always called, 'Dolly' by her family and friends.

Dolly grew into a loving happy child and then a fun-to-be with schoolgirl who was actively involved in her local church. When they started courting, Dolly made it quite clear to her young man that she was and always would be a church-going lass. Bruce Barton, being a fair-minded sort, raised no objections. He reckoned that 'church' was a good place for a woman. They were good at all that hymn singing. They could learn right from wrong in the Sunday School, sing in the choir and if they were musically inclined, and he knew that his young lady was so musically inclined, they could play the piano. But it was no place for a down-to-earth hard working man like himself.

Dolly, bless her heart, was never going to get him into any church! But she did.

On their wedding day, Bruce Barton took the beautiful, gentle and quietly spoken Verona Bloodworth to be his lawful wedded wife and he never lived to regret it. He was twenty-nine and she was twenty-seven.

They set up home together in Reservoir Road which was about three miles away from the prosperous city of Gloucester. No17 was a three-bedroomed semi-detached house and Bruce was proud to call it his own.

Their first son, Peter was born in 1930. Dolly went to stay with her mother for the confinement which was common practice in those days. Their daughter, Nita followed three years later. There was to be a twelve year gap before Dolly had her last child, Eric. A war would blight Europe and the wider world for six long weary years before he put in his appearance as it came to an end in 1945.

Nita's young life growing up in Reservoir Road was secure and uneventful. Her mother was a loving and careful home-maker. She was content, as most married women were in those pre-war days, to cook and clean and to bring up the children. Her mother's life revolved around her home and her church, Brunswick Baptist Church and the children were happy to go along with her.

Nita attended the local Infant School which was just a stone's throw from where she lived in Reservoir Road. One day she can remember coming home from school to find her mother standing on the doorstep lost in a serious conversation with a neighbour.

'It's come to it then,' said the neighbour anxiously.

'Yes, we're at war. I've just heard the news on the wireless,' said Dolly Barton.

They both shook their heads and did not greet their children returning from school with the usual happy smiles and hugs. Nita was only six and didn't really understand what was happening, but her brother Peter knew that many of his mates' fathers and brothers would be going off to fight and he wondered if his Dad would be going with them.

Bruce Barton was thirty nine years old when war broke out. He was employed in the production of Spitfires and Hurricanes up at the Gloster Aircraft Factory. This was to be his war-work as well as turning up for regular Home Guard duties which he took very seriously.

After the first initial shock and fear of possible invasion, nothing much happened and life in Reservoir Road went on as before. It looked as if the war wasn't going to amount to much after all. Then disaster struck.

Peter and Nita both contracted diphtheria. It was sweeping through the country and leaving death and destruction in its wake. It was a killer disease. Peter and Nita and many of their school friends were admitted to the Over Fever Hospital. Peter was seriously ill and his parents feared for his life. He was only ten. Nita was seven. She was ill, but it wasn't long before she became fed up with having to lie in bed all day and she hated having nothing to eat but tapioca and horrid rice pudding with skin on it.

They were not allowed any physical contact with their anxious parents who had to be content to view their loved ones through a glass partition. The Government laid down strict instructions for the care of these patients, doing all they could to prevent a wider spread of the disease. The war in 1940 was disrupting the lives of most in the country and medical staff and resources were needed to keep brave men flying Spitfires and hard pressed soldiers fighting on the front line.

Many children succumbed to the effects of that dreadful disease, but Dolly thanked God for saving the lives of her precious young ones and even her husband shed a tear or two of relief when he learned that his son had been taken off the 'Dangerously Ill' list.

When Nita's father got his children home after spending many weeks in an isolation hospital, his first instinct was to protect them. There were certain things he never wanted his children to be bothered about and the war and its awful effects was one of them. He made it his business never to have a newspaper in the house and if he came home from work and found the wireless on tuned to the Home Service of the BBC he always turned it off.

Sometimes he had to be out all night fulfilling his duties as a member of the local Home Guard. Bruce never talked about these duties in front of his children. However, it is a known fact that the Home Guard in and around Gloucester were only issued with pitchforks, but the men had no doubts at all that they would prove an effective weapon should a German invasion mean that they might have to tackle the enemy at close quarters.

Nita was especially pleased when her father had duties that kept him out all night. She was a 'mummy's girl and falling asleep in the big bed next to her dear Mother was a rare treat.

They did have an inside Morrison shelter, but Nita never remembers any of the family using it. When an air-raid was on, the children sheltered under the stairs, sometimes spending all night there and falling asleep. A few bombs were dropped up at Coney Hill where there was a RAF Records establishment, but as Reservoir Road was some distance from the city, they were able to live a relatively peaceful life.

Of course, like everyone else they had to learn to cope with the rationing of more or less everything. This is where No.17 Reservoir Road came into its own. The back garden was all of sixty feet long. There was a lawn and a couple of lilac trees screened the rest of the garden where they had blackberry bushes; blackcurrant bushes; raspberry bushes and they also grew gooseberries and rhubarb. In the vegetable garden they grew their own carrots, peas, beans, Brussels sprouts and potatoes. A Victoria plum tree meant that they had lots of delicious plums to add variety to their diet.

They had more than enough to meet their own needs so were able to barter the rest for a rabbit or two. Rabbit stew was always a great family favourite.

Nita loved helping her mother in the kitchen. It was a small kitchen by today's standards, just big enough to house a gas cooker and a boiler for the washing and a mangle. Like all her neighbours, Dolly always did her washing on Mondays in the big white china sink by hand using a scrubbing board. The ironing was done on the kitchen table using flat irons. As soon as one of the irons was piping hot, it would be put to use, while the other iron would be heating up on the gas stove ready to be called into service when the first iron cooled. The Bartons never had any hot water unless they boiled it and this meant having a bath in two or three inches of water. No fun at all in the winter!

One day there was a loud knock on the door. Dolly opened it and found a bespectacled grey-haired old man standing there holding a clip board.

'Mrs Barton, I understand you have a spare room, 'he said, without waiting for confirmation. 'It will be necessary for you to have a couple of American servicemen from the nearby USAF camp billeted on you. Of course you will be given an allowance by the Government to cover any expenses that may be incurred.'

Dolly Barton was flummoxed, speechless.

'Good! that's settled then,' said the official.' They'll be arriving in a day or two. I'm sure you'll do everything in your power to make their stay in an English home comfortable!' And then he was gone.

'It's no good. It won't do,' said her husband when he came in from work. 'I don't like it!'

'It doesn't matter whether we like it or not, 'said Dolly. 'We've just got to put up with it like the rest of Reservoir Road and make the best of it!'

'Well, you just make double sure that our Nita and Peter are kept right out of their way,' said their father. I don't want any trouble. Is that clear?'

'Well, they're only over here to help us win this wretched war, so we can give them credit for that at least!' said Dolly.

'I can always remember the day they arrived on our doorstep,' Nita said. 'It was a Saturday morning. Peter and I were at home, Dad was out. Suddenly there was a loud knock on the front door and then another knock louder than the first. Peter and I knew it had to be 'them'. Nobody else knocked on our door like that!'

Dolly showed them to the spare room which was clean and welcoming.

'If you need anything, perhaps you'll let me know,' she said. 'Once you've settled in, I'll show you the bathroom.'

One of the American soldiers reached into his kit bag and brought out a big jar of sweets. 'Please give this to your kiddies with our compliments,' he said. His friend, Hank, opened one of his bags and gave Dolly some tins of bully beef; a tin of spam; a big jar of peanut butter which she'd never seen before; some tins of powdered egg which she had; a jar of coffee; some bars of chocolate and last, but not least, some packets of Wrigley's chewing gum.

Dolly frowned. She was about to say that she couldn't possibly accept their gifts, when the tall fair-haired American G.I. said:

'Now Ma'am, please don't be offended or anything like that. It must be kinda hard trying to feed a family on the rationing you folks have over here.'

'We manage all right,' said Dolly firmly.

'Please don't get me wrong, Maam. Just take it as a gesture of friendship between our country and yours!'

124

Dolly knew that if her husband was there, he would have refused to take anything from the Americans, but she could see that they only meant to be kind, so she didn't refuse their gifts.

'Thank you,' she said. 'It's very kind of you, but please don't think you've got to keep bringing us things.'

'We won't be bothering you much at all,' they said.' We'll be up at the Camp most of the time. We'll be here to sleep and have breakfast and that's about it!'

The Americans were true to their word. The children hardly had any contact with them. They were up and away early in the morning and came home after they'd gone to bed.

Bruce Barton was like a billy goat with a sore head for a week or two after they arrived and no-one could get a civil word out of him, but when he could see that they kept themselves to themselves and didn't intrude into his family's life, he even managed a, 'morning all,' greeting when he passed them on their way to the bathroom.

And so life went on for the Bartons of Reservoir Road. There was school and regular attendance at the local Church, but there was no Brownie Pack at the C. of E. and Nita was too young for Guides, so she and her friend Joyce Winsper decided to join the Girls' Life Brigade. This meant leaving the local C. of E. church and attending Trinity Baptist Church in Finlay Road. 'It was a turning point in my young life,' said Nita. 'I settled in there very happily and never looked back.'

By the end of the war a new addition in the shape of baby brother Eric, joined the Barton family. Nita remembers the Christmas of 1945. Her uncle Sid and Auntie Ivy came to stay and her cousin June, who was also her best friend. They had great fun and frolics culminating in a family sing-song around the old piano.

Her mother played not only Christmas carols, but some other well-known favourites - 'The White Cliffs of Dover,' and 'There'll Always be an England' - songs that had kept their spirits up during the dark days of the war.

Nita left school, as most children did in those days at the age of fifteen and was bold enough to answer an advertisement for a young office worker in *GLOUCESTER CITIZEN*. She was asked to attend an interview at the Deaf and Dumb Institute. 'I got the job not really knowing very much about office work, but I ended up doing more or less everything - even looking after the superintendent's baby daughter!' said Nita.

It was 1951. Her working life was going well. Her leisure was taken up with lots of GLB activities. She had grown into a pretty amazing young lady. By the time she met a dashing young sailor at a GLB camp that summer, she was ready for excitement, adventure and Romance and with signalman Anthony Gerald Spencer, she found all three.

Peter Eric & Nita Barton

CHAPTER 17

A lull before the storm

It was late November, 1951, Tony took the train from Portsmouth to Waterloo and then went across London to Paddington to catch a train for Gloucester.

It wasn't long before he was talking to the only other occupant of his carriage.

'Hello,' he said, full of the joys of spring and excited about the prospect of seeing his lady love even though it was a wet and windy day in November.

'Hello,' replied the man who seemed a congenial sort of chap. 'Where're you off to?'

'I'm on my way to Gloucester,' said Tony cheerfully.

'So am I,' said the stranger. 'My name's Jones, what's yours?'

'Anthony Spencer, but my ship mates call me Tony. I'm a signalman in the navy,' he said proudly.

'I'm with the London City Mission,' said Douglas Jones, 'perhaps you've heard of it?'

'It's a Christian Mission working among Londoners isn't it? Have you heard of Fegan's Home for Boys by any chance?'

'I certainly have,' said the Reverend Jones. 'I've had some good times down at Stony Stratford. Are you one of Fegan's Old Boys?'

They found lots to chat about and before they knew it they had arrived in Gloucester. 'It's been nice meeting you,' said Tony as they parted, not expecting ever to see his travelling companion again. He was somewhat taken aback, therefore, when the very same Reverend Jones turned up in the pulpit of the church that he and Nita attended that Sunday morning. He was subsequently called to become the pastor of Finlay Road Baptist Church and stayed for thirty three years. It's a small world!

Once outside the station, Tony lost no time in asking a passer-by which bus he should take to get to Reservoir Road.

'If you hurry up mate, you'll just be in time to catch that No.3. That's the one you want!'

He was walking briskly up the path leading to No.15 Reservoir Road when a young man, who was walking briskly up the path to No.17 called out - 'Hi there Jack. D'yer want to see Nita?'

'Yes,' replied Tony a bit perplexed and wondering how this good-looking chap new his girl.

'Well, you're walking up the wrong garden path,' This is the one you want,' he said with a big grin all over his face.

It turned out to be Desmond King, a long-standing friend of the Bartons. Tony dutifully followed him and came to the back door of No17.

Dolly Barton was there to greet him. She was just as he had imagined. A plump white-haired motherly lady with a round face and laughing cornflower blue eyes behind her spectacles.

'Hello Tony,' she said warmly. 'We've been so looking forward to meeting you. Come in dear. Come in out of the cold.'

She took him through into the middle room to meet Nita's father who was seated in a high-backed wooden armchair smoking a Woodbine cigarette and listening to his wireless.

'Tony's arrived Dad,' said Dolly Barton. 'Look after him while I go up and tell Nita.'

Bruce Barton was a tall lean man in his early fifties. His hair was going grey and getting a bit thin on top, but he was a working man and he still had a lot of energy left in him and it showed, even while he was sitting down having a smoke.

'Hello Mr Barton,' said Tony.

'Hello young man. Sit yourself down.'

The older man looked at his daughter's sailor boy quizzically. 'Had a good journey lad?' he enquired.

'Yes sir,' Tony replied nervously.

'Well now, went into the navy at sixteen didn't you and before that Nita says you were in an orphanage. That must have been a bit rough eh?'

'Yes, it was a bit sir, but my brother and I were in there together. He's older than me and he looked out for me when I got into scrapes.'

'What about your family? I've heard about your Aunts - a stiff and starchy bunch, eh?'

'They can be awkward at times, but they mean well. Aunt Gladys took us to Canada in the war and I've always been grateful for that.'

'So now you're a navy man. I suppose the sea and ships are your passion. I'm a wood man myself. My son Peter, he's a carpenter, a craftsman. Good with his hands, good with wood. It's in the family, in the blood. D'yer like wood, Tony?'

It seemed to be an essential qualification for acceptance as a suitor for his daughter's hand. He was quick to reply.

'Oh yes sir, I like wood. I've made lots of models in wood, like a yacht that actually sailed and a plane that flew, that sort of thing when I was in Fegan's.'

'Good!' said the old man, 'and you can stop calling me 'sir'. We don't stand on ceremony in this house.

'You'd better call me 'Dad'. I've a feeling we're going to get to know each other pretty well.'

'All right, sir,' said Tony, 'I mean, Dad!'

Then Nita appeared as if she had been waiting in the wings to make her entrance. Tony stood up and they greeted each other. There was certainly something going on between these two young people, even the old man could feel it.

'I'll take you upstairs, You'll be sleeping in my brother's room,' said Nita. 'You've just missed Peter. He's in the Army and was posted overseas just a couple of days ago.'

Tony soon got to know the youngest member of the Barton family, a six year old bundle of mischief called Eric. He was a nice little boy, but a bit of a pest. When Tony tried to get a few minutes alone with Nita in the front room, he wouldn't leave them in peace even for a minute.

The week-end just flew. Dad Barton showed him his workshop which seemed as big as a barn and contained everything that a roofer could possibly need and more besides. Dolly Barton produced some scrumptiously hot meals and fussed over him, telling him to call her, 'Mum'. Eric said he couldn't wait for him to come back again to play cricket and Nita made it as clear as a freshwater trout stream that she only had eyes for him.

In December he received a draft chit informing him to join HMS *Saintes* , another battle-class destroyer in Portsmouth Dockyard. There was one last opportunity to see Nita and her family over the Christmas period and then it was all aboard *Saintes* for further adventures on the high seas. They sailed on January 1st 1952.

Tony was detailed to No.3 Mess which was down in the front part of the ship, but his job as ordinary signalman meant that he spent most of his time on the bridge or the flag deck.

He was to make some lifelong mates on *Saintes* including signalman Reg Wantling, Vic Earl and Dixie Dean a telegraphist.

Soon they were sailing into the Bay of Biscay and the most appalling weather that Tony ever hoped to encounter. He had been at sea in bad weather conditions before and was cocksure about being able to stand up to anything the elements could throw at him, but not this time.

It was as if someone had blown the lid off hell itself and tipped out the contents in the Biscay. The waves were all of fifty feet and more. Tony and his mates hadn't seen anything like it. The 3000 tonnes ship was tossed around like a paperweight. Up on the bridge as the ship reared up out of the foaming water, it seemed to hold its breath before taking the plunge once again into the raging sea. Tony found himself looking straight down into a bottomless watery grave. It was scary for a seventeen year old.

The skipper, Captain Peter Dawnay DSC, cleared everybody off the upper deck except the navigator, the chief yeoman, the signalman and the look-outs. The policy was always to get as many off the bridge as possible in a force 9 gale. Spencer happened to be the duty signalman for that watch and that was that.

There were four ships steaming in convoy, *Saintes, Vigo, Armada,* and *St. Kitts.* All four battle-class destroyers made up the 3rd Destroyer Squadron. Captain Peter Dawnay was the Squadron Commander in charge of all four ships, but each ship had its own captain. Because of the atrocious weather, the *Armada* had problems, *Saintes* had problems. *Armada* lost nearly all their lifeboats.

Seamen staggered about *Saintes* like drunken sailors as they battened down the hatches. The waves crashed down hard upon them and they slid across the deck, struggling to get the job done and escape below.

'You frightened Spencer,' enquired the skipper as he peered through his binoculars.

Trembling and shivering in his boots, the young signalman replied:

'Not half, sir!'

'So am I,' said the skipper, 'but we'll get through this lad, we'll get through it!'

Tony sincerely hoped so, but he felt less than confident as the ship plunged down into the foaming brine and rose up only to repeat the sickening process again and again. He tried to place his confidence in his skipper's certainty that they would come through this to steady his heaving stomach. He also wouldn't mind telling you that he prayed, fervently!

Suddenly a signal came on board, the Flying Enterprise, an American oil tanker was breaking up and needing assistance, but the weather was so bad *Saintes* actually passed by without even seeing it. The captain sent a signal to say that he was unable to go to its aid, but her *SOS* was picked up by an American ship, Southlades who went to her assistance and took off the ten passengers and crew with the exception of the Captain, Kurt Carlsen. The USN destroyer, John W. Weeks, also stood by.

On January 2nd a salvage tug, *Turmoil,* arrived and although the list of the Flying Enterprise had increased to eighty degrees, the tug's mate, Kenneth Dancy joined Captain Carlsen and the ship was towed towards Falmouth. Unfortunately, they were only three miles from that port when the tow parted. Captain Carlsen and Kenneth Dancy just managed to leave the damaged vessel and board the tug before the Enterprise keeled over and sank.

The storm took nearly forty eight hours to blow itself out. When they limped into Gibraltar there were obvious signs of recent damage. The jackstaff had broken off; the rails had been swept away, the heavy forward gun had been unseated by the huge waves and all the carly floats and lifeboats had been lost at sea.

While urgent repairs were being assessed and undertaken, Tony was relieved to be sent ashore to HMS *Rook* to continue his training in signals. A cushy number after what he'd been through.

In less than a week they set sail for Malta. This time the weather was great. It was plain sailing all the way. Tony was excited at the prospect of having some time in which to explore the famous George Cross Island. Soon after the ship docked, he joined his mates in the liberty boat to go ashore.

CHAPTER 18

MALTA - January 1952

Tony was excited at the prospect of having time ashore to explore the famous George Cross Island.

'Why is Malta called the George Cross Island, sir?' he asked Yeoman Harvey. 'The George Cross is a civilian medal, but the people of Malta were defending their island in war-time weren't they?'

'Yes Spencer, you're right, but because they were civilians defending their island home against all that the enemy could throw at them without surrendering is the very reason they were awarded it!'

Yeomen Harvey, Soden, Parker and Riddington were in their thirties. Some of them still had vivid memories of those dark days. They were happy to be returning to Malta now that the war years were in the past. But they would never be forgotten by the people of Malta or by the navy veterans who had survived them.

'Reg, who's that calling? Is it Lascaris?' enquired Tony of his mate.

'Yep. There they are. We're just getting into Malta and blow me if they're not getting us on signals already!'

'Look at the capital ships over there on the left. What's he doin'? He's turning. Are we going back out again?' 'No,' said Reg. 'He's turned the ship round. We're reversing. Look at that line of buoys. I hope we don't hit 'em. The buoy jumpers are out. Yep, there they go securing a chain.' 'Ern, whereabouts are we? What's that place over there?'

'That's Manoel Island. That's where you'll go ashore to do your signal training and that sort of thing.'

'But what's that big place right over there?'

'Oh, that'll be HMS *Forth*. She's a submarine depot ship, but you won't need to go there.'

'It's so bloomin' hot,' said Tony mopping his brow. If only they could see us back home now. I bet they're knee deep in snow and battling against icy winds!'

The next day, Tony and Reg boarded the liberty boat which took them round to Sliema Creek and dropped them off by the 'England Forever' bar.

'How much money have you got on you?' asked Tony.

'Two and six.'

'I've got a quid,' said Tony. 'That should be enough.' They sauntered along the harbour and found a café that served up a big juicy steak, egg and chips and loads of bread and butter for the princely sum of 9d. Tony was well pleased. Reg ordered a big plate of fish, chips and peas - it went down a treat and only set him back 6d.

'We're going to do all right here,' said Reg. 'We won't go hungry that's for sure,' said Tony.

They watched HMS *Vigo* come in. 'What a mess she made of coming down compared to what our skipper did,' said Tony.

'What else can you expect from the last ship of the group,' said Reg with a shrug of his big shoulders. But for these men there was just no competition, HMS *Saintes* took the biscuit every time. Eventually they found themselves in Floriana where Tony discovered a Methodist Church and right next door the Connaught - a rest home and club for all service personnel on the Island. They went in and Tony recognised one of the men.

'George, George Cruz isn't it?'

'Hello Tony,' said George. 'You know my pal Ken don't you?'

They were R.A.F. boys, but when off duty and ashore, the R.A.F. and navy boys would all meet up at the Connaught for social events. There were barn dances on Saturday nights and swimming parties out in St. Paul's Bay or at Golden Sands. But they had only one thing on their minds when not on duty - girls, girls - pretty girls!

It didn't take long for his mess mates on board *Saintes* to discover that Spencer was a firm teetotaller. Sometimes they were even thankful for it. When they went ashore hell bent on having a 'skinful', he would be sure to meet up with them at the end of the day when half of them would be dead drunk and the rest as high as a kite. Inevitably they would need the good services of a fit young man to assist them as they tried to negotiate the narrow gangplank.

Tony spent most of his time ashore sight-seeing, swimming or playing hockey whenever he could get the chance. Amazingly he managed to keep cheerful and have a good time without frequenting bars or hitching up with any of the local talent. This had the effect of riling some of his shipmates. They became determined to initiate him into the wicked ways of the big wide world before he got any older - by hook or by crook!

In Valetta there was a well known haunt of men looking for women and booze, Straight Street, but more commonly known by it's notorious name, 'the Gut'. It was situated in the red-light district. If you were a sailor, you walked down this street with fear and trepidation. The ladies of the night, who frequented the Gut would endeavour to persuade sailors to sample their wares with a saucy look and a lewd invitation, but if their charms failed, they would resort to strong-arm tactics. They'd grab hold of the unguarded and drag them into their dark dwellings. It was rumoured - they were never seen alive again!

Some of the sailors who had not been unwilling victims, longed to witness the moral downfall of the young and wet-behind-the-ears signalman, Spencer. The upright, clean living, Bible bashing, blue eyed 'mummy's' boy!

They plotted and planned how to achieve their nefarious aim and then set to work. One day they were in the Mess chatting among themselves, when young and cocky Derek Miles, threw down the gauntlet. It took the form of a dare. A challenge was hard to resist among the men without leaving oneself open to the unattractive charge of being 'chicken' or even worse, a sheer coward. Even the most timid sailor was always prevailed upon to take up the challenge, because the alternative was unthinkable.

'You could do it, couldn't you Tony?' said Miles. 'Do what?' asked Tony who hadn't been paying much attention to the jokes and banter.

'You could walk with us down the Gut and not be taken in by any of the beautiful seductive ladies seeking the companionship of a poor young sailor, like yourself couldn't you?'

'What?' said Tony. 'No thanks. I think I'll pass on that one.' But his mess mates were not going to let him off the hook so easily. They pressed him.

'Come on Spencer. You just have to walk down it, not go with any of them. Perhaps you don't think you could say 'No,' eh?'

'Saying 'No!' wouldn't be too difficult,' said Tony laughing.

'Well, we'll have to see about that, won't we boys!' said Miles triumphantly. Now he'd got Spencer just where he wanted him.

Bets flew back and forth. 'Ten bob says he'll give in - ten bob says he won't. Let's see the colour of your money!'

It was no good Tony protesting. He had said that it wouldn't be too difficult to say 'No', now he had to be man enough to prove it!

'What about that!' he said to Reg Wantling later when he came off watch. 'Suppose they drag me into one of their hovels?'

'You'd better pray to God they don't, me lad because believe me, if they do, you'll never live to tell the tale!'

'Oh come off it. It can't be that bad,' said Tony, trying to reassure himself.

'It's that bad!' said Reg.

'Oh,' said Tony with a worried look on his face. It doesn't look as if I'm going to be able duck out of this one!' 'No,' said Reg, 'not without a lynching!' The following Saturday night, all bets were on. A whole gang of sailors made sure that young Spencer was in their boozy company when they made for Straight Street. Tony was very nervous although he was bravely flanked by his best pals Reg and Vic.

'You hang on to us for dear life,' they said, 'and we'll hold on to you. And whatever you do, don't stop or say anything to them or they'll have your guts for garters! Cheer up Tony. You only die once!'

The other ratings were in great form. Laughing and shouting at the top of their voices. 'Come on, Spencer, let's 'have yer.' Tonight was going to be great sport!

Tony, Reg and Vic soon found themselves surrounded by sailors who were determined to win their bet. They sauntered and swayed down the Gut already much the worse for drink. It wasn't long before they were accosted by the ladies of the night.

'Come on darling. Let me give you a good time, eh? You come here with me. Come on, darling!' said one to Reg.

'No thanks mate,' he answered and kept walking on mindful of his bounden duty to protect his friend.

'My name's Maria. You are a good-looking sailor. I like you very much. You come, have a drink with me,' said another to Vic.

'Not tonight Josephine,' said Vic, smiling in spite of himself.

Tony doggedly kept on walking. It was difficult. When the whole gang slowed down, he was forced to go at a snail's pace.

'Keep going mate,' urged Vic. 'Whatever you do don't fall over or you're dead meat!'

Suddenly there was a not so young woman in front of him. 'I like you young boy,' she said. 'You come with me eh?'

'Not on your life,' said Tony with a shudder. He was hating every minute of this 'adventure' and it completely finished him when another sailor stopped the forward momentum to be violently sick.

'That does it,' he said angrily to his companions. 'I'm getting out of this hell hole!' He marched forward for the remaining thirty yards or so and it was all over bar the shouting.

'Home and dry!' said Vic.

'Thank God for that!' replied Tony mightily relieved. He had realized once and for all what he wasn't missing when he didn't join his shipmates who regularly got themselves drunk and later boasted of their conquests among the ladies. He didn't need it. He had found something, Someone better!

It must be said though that some of his shipmates did meet up with and eventually marry some of the beautiful young very devout church-going Maltese girls and lived happily ever after, but Tony wasn't one of these. He went on dreaming of his Nita back home in England and eagerly awaited her heart-warming letters, confident that she was waiting for him.

Nita Barton wasn't the only one in her family writing letters to a member of the forces serving overseas. Dolly Barton was busy writing to her son, Peter asking him to look out for Tony Spencer.

By the summer of 1952, Peter Barton was a national serviceman serving with the Royal Berkshire Rifle Regiment and stationed in the Suez Canal Zone, along with some 80,000 British soldiers. They were housed under canvass and because political relations with Egypt had taken a turn for the worse, no Egyptian workers were employed which meant all the menial jobs were allotted to the army.

The flies, the dirt and the oppressive heat meant morale among the rank and file was at a low ebb when an incident occurred involving anti-British Egyptian natives resulting in the deaths of some soldiers on guard duty, making matters even worse. It became imperative for the Army to arrange frequent breaks to and from Cyprus to give the men a much needed breather. This was how Peter Barton happened to be in Cyprus with a couple of his mates when HMS *Saintes* sailed into port.

'Hi there mate.. Would you happen to know a sailor by the name of Tony Spencer?' enquired Peter Barton hopefully.

'Nope, never heard of him,' said the sailors and got on with their drinking. It was hot in Famagusta - drinking weather.

Peter Barton continued his search accompanied by his best mate, Tony Quinlan. He was determined to find him before he was shifted back to Suez.

Eventually it got back to Tony that a soldier was asking after him. Tony was curious. What was that all about he wondered. Who was he and what was he after? He was due some shore leave and assigned to a station in Cyprus while his ship took off for foreign parts.

'I could get used to this sort of life,' said Tony to his mates while sitting outside a café knocking back an ice Coke and soaking up the sun.

Just then a couple of soldiers approached them looking decidedly shifty Tony thought. Sort of on the prowl.

'Anyone of you know a sailor by the name of Tony Spencer?' enquired one of them.

'Who wants to know?' said Tony cautiously.

'Why, do you know him,' said Peter Barton.

'I ought to know him,' said Tony grinning. 'It's me.'

'About time. I've been looking for you all over the place,' said Peter wiping the sweat from his brow. ''I'm Peter Barton, Nita's brother!'

'Well, stone me!' said Tony. 'I'd heard a soldier was bandying my name about, but I'd no idea it was Nita's brother. Sit down and have a drink. What are you doing in Cyprus anyway? I heard you were with the Suez lot.'

'It was a turn up for the book, meeting Peter like that,' said Tony. 'It somehow made Nita seem that much closer. We became good mates and went all over the island sight-seeing together.

All too soon this happy interlude came to an end. Peter and his pals of the Royal Berkshires reluctantly returned to the dust, dirt and flies of Suez. But Tony and his mates had no such reluctance when it came to rejoining their good ship, HMS *Saintes* and setting sail for more adventures upon the high seas.

Anthony in 1953

Straight Street - Malta

CHAPTER 19

Saints Alive!

HMS *Saintes* patrolled the Suez Canal stopping off at Lake Timsa. Then they sailed down to Suez itself. Port Said is at one end of the Canal and Suez the other. There was a big army camp at Moaska and the crew were given the chance of going ashore. This gave Tony another opportunity of meeting up with Peter Barton.

There was trouble afoot in Egypt. Revolutionary elements in the Egyptian army threatened even the throne and King Farouk was ousted. This had far-reaching effects for the British in the region. 'The Suez Canal will run red with English blood!' Col.Nasser announced to the world press. 'The English had better get out while they still have the chance.' As a consequence British troops were deployed in strength on the ground and the British navy patrolled the Suez Canal to keep it open and safe for international shipping. It was a very uneasy time. No-one knew when Nasser would strike.

It was getting hot in Cyprus too and it wasn't just the weather. The Turks and Greeks who inhabited the island were becoming restless and looking for a political way out in which to settle their deep differences. This was all under ground in the early 1950s, but the signs were there and British servicemen stationed in Cyprus had to be on their guard.

Saintes continued it's tour of service in Suez, Cyprus and Malta interposed with fleet exercises to keep the men on their toes. They were also deployed to visit various friendly nations on a goodwill mission. In this way Tony was able to see quite a lot of the world: Beirut, Instanbul, Athens, Rome and Trieste. He even managed to get off the ship with some of his mates and hitch a ride in a landrover to Cairo. It must be said that he wasn't taken with Egypt. It was dirty. Too much sand. Too many flies.

On one particular occasion they were given a tour of the desert. Surprisingly they came across a little Foreign Legion Outpost. Even there they found the natives selling their wares - miles away from the populace and with very little hope of customers suddenly turning up out of the blue. Tony was taken with some silver bracelets.

'You like it?' enquired a wizened old man. 'For you, for your wife?'

'For my girl, perhaps,' he said.

A crowd soon gathered around them, chattering cajolling, persuading the young British sailors to buy. Tony eventually succumbed and paid the asking price which was much more than they had hoped to receive. They were triumphant and rejoiced at this unexpected largesse.

'They were just a bunch of poor Arabs living in a small village in the desert,' he said. Tony's 'girl' still treasures that silver bracelet.

However, not all the natives were friendly. In Trieste there was trouble. The crew were invited to an army camp and were told to go in one entrance and to be careful to exit from that same entrance. Some of the lads turned out from the camp using another exit. Straight away they found themselves in a forbidden military zone surrounded by armed hostile solders who arrested them. Some of the ship's company were forcibly detained. It was no easy matter for the ship's captain to get them released when a charge of 'spying' had been levelled against them!

On another occasion they visited Tobruk in North Africa on a courtesy visit. The ship's company wondered at the explosions they could hear coming from the mainland. 'It's either people or goats stepping on landmines,' said one of the officers. Nevertheless, the intrepid young signalman, Spencer and other interested parties were allowed ashore, but were warned to keep their wanderings to the flagged areas where the land had been cleared of mines. Tony was keen to visit Torbruk because it had been made famous in the Second World War by Field Marshal Montgomery and his daring Desert Rats. The British 8th Army had confronted Rommel and his tank divisions and routed them!

When the men returned on board unscathed, there was an uncharacteristic pall of heaviness hanging over the crew, a definite absence of the usual hustle and bustle and cheerful camaraderie that was a feature of the ship's daily life. Then they were given the news. King George VI had died.

'Yes, it did have an effect on all of us,' said Tony. 'All the men held the King and Queen Elizabeth in high regard and were genuinely saddened at the King's early death. We knew he would be missed, not only by his family, but by the nation, by the Commonwealth, by all the men and women in His Majesty's services.'

All the warships on duty in the Mediterranean were positioned under the flight path of the plane carrying the young Queen Elizabeth and Prince Philip back from Kenya and arrangements were made to ensure the Queen's safety should anything unforeseen happen during the flight. But all went well. The new Queen was only twenty six years of age at the time. She had gone out to Kenya a Princess not knowing that when she returned she would be Queen of the United Kingdom and the British Commonwealth of nations.

Early in 1953 *Saintes* was en route to Malta cruising in the Mediterranean when a distress signal was received on board - 'MAYDAY! MAYDAY! MAYDAY!' Tony learned that a Valetta aircraft returning from Egypt had crashed into the sea. A small American Airforce amphibious plane that happened to be in the area was first on the scene, but signalled to *Saintes* for help to rescue the survivors.

The boarding party hastily set out with Tony Spencer as signalman in a whaler towing two carly floats in which to transport the survivors. When they reached the American seaplane they found it covered by the men, women and children who had been picked up out of the sea. They were on the wings, on the fuselage and even hanging onto the tail of the plane.

'It's great to see you guys!' shouted the American airman when the boarding party arrived. 'I'm stuck here and can't take off with all these folks sitting on my tail!'

'Come along,' said Tony to the very wet and weary passengers, some of them children. 'Here, take my hand. We'll soon have you off and safely away!'

They were not all eager to leave the wings and fuselage of the small plane, afraid of falling into the sea again, but some of the men among the survivors were able to persuade the women to get close enough to grab the hands of the British sailors who had been sent to rescue them.

'That's right,' encouraged Tony. 'Move along and into the carly floats behind the whaler.' They edged nervously forward and one by one were taken off the seaplane. One of the children was quite distraught. She had lost her teddy.

They had to make a couple of trips back and forth to *Saintes* because they could only transport twenty passengers at any one time. Suddenly the wind got up and very quickly the sea became treacherous. Tony, who was holding on to the bows of the whaler was roughly thrust into the fuselage of the stranded aircraft, seriously injuring his right arm - although he didn't realise it at the time.

He managed with some difficulty to wrench his injured arm free from the wrecked plane and get back into the whaler. It was time he signalled *Saintes*. Unable to use his right arm which was hanging limp and useless at his side, he put the Aldis lamp into the crook of his arm and signalled using his left:

'All survivors taken off damaged plane. Plane unable to take off. Will endeavour to tow back.'

All thirty six survivors were eventually taken aboard *Saintes*. They were traumatized and suffering from shock, but there was no loss of life. In the meantime, conditions became so bad that even though they tried to tow the damaged American plane to safety, it proved to be impossible.

When the American pilot could see that there was nothing more that he could do to save his plane, he reluctantly agreed to leave it and joined the British sailors in the whaler. He was only just in time. A heavy squall caused the little plane to lift its nose out of the water for one last time and then it was lost beneath the waves.

When it came to getting back on board *Saintes*, Tony had great difficulty trying to grab hold of the rope ladder at the side of the ship. He was pushed up from below and hauled up from above - a painful procedure. He was transferred to Sick Bay, not quite sure what he'd done to his right arm, but by then it was black and blue and swollen up to twice its normal size. A sick berth attendant quipped:

'This arm looks like a dog's dinner, Spencer. We'll probably have to cut it off!' This really put the wind up Tony and he wasn't reassured when the ship's medical officer took one look at it and added:

'What a mess! I can't fix it on board *Saintes*. You'll have to go ashore Spencer!'

As soon as the ship had got the rescued passengers safely transported to a shore base, they sailed for Cyprus. Tony would have to be treated at the RAF hospital in Nicosia.

'I had an awful scare when we got there,' he said. 'We were told at the gates of RAF Nicosia that we were expected and to go to the third Nissen hut on the left. We did, but it was locked. We couldn't get in. I wondered what on earth was going on. We went around the side and opened a door into what was obviously an operating theatre. You'll never believe it, but there lying forlornly on the theatre table was some poor devil's recently amputated arm! That was enough for me,' Tony said. 'I took off. You couldn't see me for dust!'

The whole camp was alerted and a search party sent out to scour the hospital grounds for one seriously injured absconding sailor. After they found him, no matter how much he protested, he was escorted back to that same operating theatre.

A very famous surgeon, Sir Archibald McIndoe, who worked in the RAF burns unit, took one look at signalman Spencer's arm and said menacingly:

'Ah yes. I've always wanted to get my hands on a sailor!'

'Look here sir,' Tony ventured. 'Please go easy on my arm. I've grown rather attached to it.'

'We'll have to see about that young man,' smirked the great man. And that was the last thing he knew before he was given a general anaesthetic and went under the surgeon's knife.

He did not lose his arm, but he was in plaster for months. Apparently his semaphore signalling with a stiff right arm was a thing of beauty. Fred Cornish on one of the sister ships in the flotilla recalls:

'I could always tell when it was Tony signalling. Up went his damaged arm dead straight. He appeared to be jerked into action as if someone up above was pulling his strings. It was quite a comical sight!'

Signalman Spencer took it all in his stride. He was happy to be back on board ship and doing his job with a stiff arm rather than being shore based.

Everything was going along when disaster struck was September 10th 1953. A terrible earthquake devastated Paphos on the island of Cyprus. Hundreds of Greek and Turkish-Cypriot homes were ruined. Ktima and scores of villages throughout the district were completely destroyed.

Saintes and other ships in the region were soon at the scene to bring what relief and assistance they could to the suffering civilian population. Once again Tony, now able-bodied, was assigned as signalman of the boarding party and was sent ashore to establish a communications centre.

This was the first time that he had witnessed the chaos and devastation an earthquake wreaks on an unsuspecting and unprepared civilian population. 'It was absolutely awful,' he recalls. 'There were women crying out beside themselves with grief, trying to dig out their sons and daughters from the rubble of their homes with their bare hands.'

The sailors set to work straight away helping to bring out the injured.

Meanwhile the navy doctor and his team soon had an emergency medical tent set up and running.

Tony's main job was of course to set up signal bases. One of these was installed on top of an old house. It appeared to be safe because there was so much rubble and masonry on the site.

As they worked away, Tony and his mates saw a road leading away from the old ruined house.

'We navy lads noticed a little boy running along the road and a young girl who appeared to be following him, walking some distance behind. Suddenly, all hell broke loose. There was a terrifying rumbling noise which grew louder and louder. We could see the earth all around shaking and moving. It frightened the living daylights out of us. Then the road on which we had seen the little girl walking just opened up and closed again. The poor little girl was gone. We stared at each other in disbelief,' said Tony. 'We were speechless. We couldn't do a thing about it!'

The lads didn't break down or throw up. They were there as navy men in uniform, professionally trained to take orders and do their job. Never far from their thoughts was the honourable tradition handed down from Lord Nelson:

'England expects every man to do his duty' - whatever the circumstances. Their first duty was to their captain, to carry out his orders. This enabled them to distance themselves from the horrors of what they were witnessing and to get on with the task at hand. They knew it was essential to establish communication between Paphos and *Saintes*.

Tony was soon able to send the Medical Officer's message requesting blankets, more tents and further medical supplies and he and his team were gratified when some big Land Rovers turned up bringing what was desperately needed.

It subsequently took a lot of time and effort from many agencies to bring the situation back to anything like normality. The death toll was forty, but hundreds of Turkish and Greek Cypriots were injured and rendered homeless and would need help for a long time after the event.

Eventually *Saintes* was relieved and set sail for Malta where her crew were due a well earned rest.

That Christmas, Tony received parcels not only from his aunts, but from his dear Nita. Her letters were a lifeline to him. At last he had found his own young lady who cared about him. They both looked forward to 1954 when his tour of service abroad would be at an end. He would be going home good old Blighty. He was a sailor and he loved the sea, but he'd found another love and his future was that much more exciting and wonderful because of it.

Air-Sea Rescue

CHAPTER 20

The Empire Windrush

It was March 1954. *Saintes* had been visiting Algiers showing the flag and was on its way back to Gibraltar for re-provisioning when one of the 'sparkers' picked up a distress signal from the which was a troopship in the Med on her way back to Southampton.

'*MAYDAY! MAYDAY!* Serious fire in engine room.'

Everybody on board *Saintes* had heard of the *Windrush*. It had made the headlines in every national paper in the UK in 1948 when she had docked in Tilbury bringing hundreds of jolly Jamaican migrants to work in Great Britain. At that time, she was feted and the migrants were welcomed with open arms. They were needed to fill the huge gap in the labour market brought about by the devastation of World War II and the aftermath of a Britain still in the grip of rationing and surrounded by the debris of bombed out buildings.

HMS *Saintes* received the order from the Flagship in the Med to go to her aid specifically to take her in tow for passage to Algiers.

'What's up?' enquired Reg Wantling when he saw his mate Tony Spencer hurrying around the ship with instructions for each of the various departments.

'We're off,' replied Tony. 'The *Empire Windrush* is in trouble. Explosion in the engine room. Four poor devils killed.'

More information was coming into *Saintes* all the time. Fire was raging on board. The troopship was carrying over a thousand personnel, including women and children. They were abandoning ship. The situation was critical.

'We got to her and saw right away that she was burning fiercely,' recalls Tony. 'The sea was choppy and dotted about all over the place where lifeboats filled with women and children. Some men still on board were in the act of jumping ship. It was that bad. Rescue ships from five nations were standing by to pick up survivors.'

When the captain gave the order - 'Boarding party away,' - four seaman, including Tony Spencer and Lt. Rivet-Carnac, boarded one of the whalers and were soon scrambling aboard the *Empire Windrush*. 'When we got on board, it was apparent that the centre section of the ship was completely gutted, but was still smouldering and steam was rising along the waterline amidships,' recalls Tony. 'Both masts were still standing, but the after funnel had collapsed and the forward funnel was inclined at a drunken angle. The ship was listing to starboard. It was a sad sight to see such destruction and desolation.'

The boarding party worked fast to secure towing wire to cable before the forecastle became enveloped in smoke and flames and the tow was completed with three shackles of cable from *Saintes*.

'I was up in the bows,' Tony said 'when in the midst of all that confusion, I found an officer's cap containing a camera, a wallet and a watch. It was as if he had tucked it in under the bows for safekeeping and forgot them when deciding to jump. I hoped to God he had made it to safety!'

'We set to battening down the hatches to contain the fire,' said Tony. 'I signalled to *Saintes* what was happening, *Saintes* signalled back, 'You've got flames coming from the stern,' so the lads hurried to the stern to contain it. Then we let an anchor chain go to stabilize the ship. It seemed that as fast as we closed one door, flames would burst out of another. It was really scary,' said Tony. 'The heat and smoke were suffocating.'

Suddenly there was a loud explosion. The men instinctively ducked and got their heads down. The ship's safe had blown. There was money flying about all over the place. 'It was a strange sight,' recalls Tony. 'I collected what I could and stuffed it into the officer's cap to be handed in as soon as I returned to my ship. Then we received the signal from *Saintes* - 'abandon ship, abandon ship!'

Because the *Windrush* was a famous ship, the press was out in full force. As the boarding party scrambled down the rope ladder into the waiting whaler, photographers from the *DAILY MIRROR* and the *MAIL* took pictures that were seen by Nita Barton and her family at home in Gloucester long before Tony had had a chance to write and tell her about it and reassure her that he was OK.

Soon after mid-day, *Saintes* started towing the *Windrush* heading for Gibraltar. The weather was fine and the tow proceeded satisfactorily during daylight hours, but as the day wore on, the fires took on a new lease of life. Smoke was seen pouring from the whole length of the ship. After dark, flames were visible and the *Windrush* became unmanageable. Her list increased and shortly after midnight on March 30th 1954 the bow suddenly rose high out of the water and by the light of searchlights was seen to slide beneath the surface. As she disappeared, *Saintes* slipped the tow. *Saintes'* crew witnessed her departure with sadness knowing that four brave men had lost their lives in her service.

Later, when Tony had an opportunity to write to his dear Nita, he mentioned *Saintes* involvement in seeking to tow the *Empire Windrush* to safety, but then went on to say:

'About this being the last cruise of the commission dearest and how do I feel about it - well, I am excited about coming home. It seems ages since I left England.'

From the end of March right up to nearly the end of May, the ship's company were kept busy showing the flag and engaged in Fleet exercises, but at last the day dawned when HMS *Saintes* sailed into Portsmouth Harbour. She had returned to port after an absence of two and a half years in foreign parts.

There on the quay to greet him were his aunts, Sylvia and Emily looking a bit shy and standing a little apart from them was Nita.

There were hugs and kisses all round, but it transpired that the Aunts had already arranged for Tony to go back with them to London. He was supposed to stay with Aunt Gladys for the week-end and to spend a longer time with Aunts Sylvia and Emily. It looked as if Nita was going to be left out in the cold.

'I'm sorry aunts,' said Tony manfully, 'but my first week of leave is already promised. I'm going up to Gloucester to spend it with Nita and her family!'

There were loud protests and hurtful remarks about Tony being an 'ungrateful wretch,' but Tony had made his mind up and would brook no further interference in his arrangements. The aunts took off for London without him and Tony and Nita were left to hold hands and talk their heads off as they made their way by train up to Gloucester.

It was a wonderful reunion. Mr and Mrs Barton treated Tony like a long lost son. Peter Barton was home and was pleased to meet up with him again and even young Eric looked upon Tony as a bit of a hero, having learned of his exploits aboard HMS *Saintes* and seen proof of it in the newspapers.

All too soon it was time to leave Nita and the Bartons and travel up to do his duty by his aunts. They had written to him often while he was away at sea and sent him parcels of goodies to keep his spirits up. He knew that they had been there for him and his brother ever since he could remember and had stood in for absent and dysfunctional parents although Tony still had doubts about that being true of his father.

The week in London flashed by. He was very impressed by his brother who was a natty dresser and quite the man about town. He had returned to Hiscock & Appleby after finishing his national service in the R.A.F., but did not anticipate spending the rest of his life with the firm. He was serious about wanting to branch out and start his own business.

Tony left London and made his way to HMS *Mercury* which was a Royal Navy School of Signals situated in Hampshire for 'sparkers' and 'bunting tossers'. While stationed there, he had an opportunity to take care of some unfinished business. He had discovered that the officer, whose effects he had rescued from the *Windrush,* lived in a village near *Mercury* and was encouraged by his superior officer to return them personally.

On his day off, looking as smart as sixpence in his best Royal Navy uniform, he set off carefully carrying his booty to the address he had been given in East Meon. It was a beautiful summer's day in June. There were blue skies overhead, a gentle breeze, the lark was on the wing, the snail on the thorn, God was in heaven, all was right with the world.

'Come in, come in,' said a beautiful grey-haired older lady when he knocked on the door. She was surprised and delighted to receive a navy man into her home, especially as he seemed to know her grandson who was a serving officer in the merchant navy.

'My grandson isn't here at the moment,' she said apologetically, 'but he'll be back shortly.' 'I know he'll be happy to meet you! It's such a lovely day. Let's go out in the garden and I'll ask Doris to bring us some tea!'

The good old British standby for every situation, 'a cup of tea'. 'Yes, that would be nice,' he said.

The garden was spacious and welcoming leading down to a stream. She showed him around. It was obviously her domain. She loved it. She was a gardener.

'Do you garden?' she enquired of her visitor.

'No ma'am,' he replied. 'I'm away at sea most of the time, but I'd like to when I can get myself settled down.'

He felt quite at home with his charming host and was almost disappointed when her Merchant navy grandson turned up with his mother. They were both very surprised to find a young naval signalman being entertained to tea and home-made scones in the garden.

Tony stood up and was about to explain what he was doing there when he was interrupted.

'This young man is stationed down at HMS *Mercury*,' said his grandmother. 'He's come on a goodwill mission bearing gifts.'

This didn't really do much for the puzzled listeners and they looked at Tony for further explanation.

'Well sir,' said Tony addressing the young officer, 'I was with the boarding party from HMS *Saintes* on the *Empire Windrush* before she went down in the Med and found certain things belonging to you and I've just come to return them,' and with that he presented the young man with the cap, the camera, the wallet and the watch almost ceremoniously as if discharging a sacred duty.

The young merchant navy officer was speechless. He had given up hope of ever seeing his things again. He took hold of the watch and to Tony's embarrassment there were tears in his eyes.

'This is a very special watch,' he told Tony. 'It was a gift from my family for my 21st birthday. It's an old family heirloom that's been in the family and passed from father to son for a long time. I'm so happy to see it again!'

After that it became talk of the sea and ships. The ladies left the sailors to it and took a walk around the garden.

Tony left knowing that he had played a small part in bringing something that was irreplaceable back to where it belonged. For a short time he had been part of a family where each generation was esteemed and had a vital role to play in the well-being and happiness of them all.

This is what he would remember about that occasion, and this is what they gave to him. A picture of what life was meant to be about. He resolved from then on to do what he could in the future to be a family man.

Empire Windrush on fire

CHAPTER 21

'To be or not to be?'

Signalman Anthony Gerald Spencer was drafted from HMS *Mercury* to HMS *Victory* in 1954. He was stationed in the Central Signal station which is the semaphore tower in the Royal Naval Dockyard Portsmouth and Gilkicker station in Lee-on-Solent.

He was enthusiastic about his new job in the semaphore tower - sending signals to the fleet in the dockyard and reporting on all the shipping entering or leaving the port. Every morning he would send a 'biffer' - an exercise in flashing and semaphore to young signalmen learning their trade.

His job in Gilkicker Station was a very important one. When the merchant ships coming in passed the NAB Tower, signals were sent requesting their name and country of origin. This information was then forwarded to Southampton Docks as they passed Gilkicker point. The port authorities were then able to organise gangs of stevedores to be ready to receive the ships and unload their cargo. In the past dockers would be waiting around all day for ships to come in. It was a time of great cooperation between the Royal Navy and the Merchant Navy.

In August Tony was granted some leave and was very excited about having a holiday with his girl friend. They decided on Eastbourne. A Christian youth conference was taking place in the town and they planned to attend. The week was taken up attending rallies and workshops, but Tony became disgruntled because he was longing to spend more time alone with Nita. They were constantly surrounded by crowds of young people. Nita didn't seem to mind. She was really enjoying herself.

When they arrived back in Gloucester at the end of the week, Tony was in a bit of a mood. Nita couldn't make out what was making him irritable. She made a casual remark about it being a beautiful summer evening and Tony snapped her head off.

'What's the matter Tony?' she said, wondering what she had done to upset her sailor boy friend. Perhaps he was wanting to end their friendship and this was his way of letting her know.

'I don't know what you mean,' he said crossly. 'Nothing's the matter! This is our last night together, we might as well go out for a stroll before we say goodnight.'

Tony took the path that led along the canal and for a while said nothing. Nita followed a step or two behind. Suddenly they heard a loud snorting noise out in front of them. They looked at each other puzzled. Nita drew closer to Tony. 'Whatever is it?' she said nervously. It certainly seemed to be getting too close for comfort. Tony suddenly grabbed hold of Nita's hand and they both jumped off the path and into the dense undergrowth.

The wild 'snorting' animal appeared briefly and thundered past. It wasn't a raging bull on the war path as Tony had half expected, but a brindled old cow who was panicking in her efforts to be reunited with the herd.

'Well,' laughed Tony. 'I didn't exactly rescue you from a fate worse than death did I?'

'No,' said Nita, 'but I must admit I was very nervous and glad you grabbed hold of me and got us off the path.' Tony looked at Nita lying amidst the ferns and brambles, and carefully removed some foliage from her hair. He didn't want to spoil the moment by helping her up on to her feet. He bent over and kissed her tenderly. He had been longing to do that all the week. She was warm and responsive. He kissed her again and again. At last he helped her to her feet and held her tight for the last time. He never wanted to let her go.

'Nita,' he whispered in her ear, what do you think about marrying a young sailor who's mad about you?'

'Well, I don't know,' she teased. 'I'll have to think about it!'

'Then you don't care for me after all,' he said, as if he hadn't really believed that this girl he was so in love with could possibly love him in return.

'Don't be so silly. I do care,' she said. 'And I want to marry you Tony!'

He took her in his arms again. 'Just for a minute there you had me worried,' he said.

They hurried back home to Reservoir Road. 'Mum, Dad, Tony has asked me to marry him and I've said yes,' Nita blurted out. 'We're engaged!'

At the end of 1955 Tony received a draft chit to go to HMS *Duchess*, a Daring-class destroyer. This meant he would be going abroad again for a further two and a half years. He told Nita about it and they decided to get married before he went.

Nita told her Mum. She was happy about it, but worried that they had less than a month to get the dress made, and set up all the other arrangements for the wedding. Tony was due to leave with his ship on February 21st. The only fly in the ointment was Nita's father. He was the next port of call for Tony to specifically ask him for his daughter's hand in marriage. Bruce Barton was a stickler for doing things properly and Tony knew that he had his work cut out to win him over.

'Hello Dad,' said Tony, one chilly January evening. 'Can I have a word?'

'We'll go into the front room,' said Nita's father. 'We'll get a bit of peace and quiet there.'

They both sat down. Tony felt very uneasy. He eyed the picture on the wall above Bruce Barton's head depicting a young Edwardian couple holding hands and standing in the hallway outside a study where an older man was seated writing at his desk.

It seemed to him that they were in the same predicament as himself. The picture was entitled, 'To be or not to be?' Yes, thought Tony. That was the question!

Bruce Barton offered Tony a cigarette and lit one himself. Then he opened the conversation by talking about the weather; the state of the country and then the work of being a roofer. He just went on and on and on. Tony couldn't get a word in edgeways. After a couple of hours, Tony couldn't take any more. He wondered if Nita's father was being deliberately obstructive.

'Look here Dad,' he said, 'I've come to ask you if I can marry Nita?' There he'd said it. Now Dad would have to give him an answer.

'You took your time about it, young man!' quipped her father. 'So you two young people want to get married do you? Well, you're both too young. You've no place to bring a bride to and you'd be going away to sea and leaving her behind with her family. What's the point of that? I say wait. There's no hurry. It'll be high time when Nita is twenty seven or twenty eight. I'll not give my consent before then. It's no good you saying anything. My mind's made up,' and with that he took out a big white handkerchief and blew his nose loudly.

'We'll have to see about that,' said Tony. 'Nita wants to marry me before I sail in February. Mum is happy about it. Nita is over twenty-one, Dad!'

This made Bruce Barton hopping mad. 'If you've got it all plotted and planned behind me back,' he said, 'I don't know why on earth you bothered to ask me for my permission!' He got up, pulled on his coat, grabbed his hat and stormed out of the house.

Well, that was not at all the way Tony had planned it. Now he wasn't sure how Nita and her Mum would take Dad's refusal to give his consent.

'Not to worry,' said Mum Barton. 'He won't like it, but he'll come round. He wouldn't miss his only daughter's wedding for the world. You'll see!' Dolly Barton was right and Tony and Nita were married on February 11th 1956. Godfrey Spencer turned up with the ring in his pocket and a big grin on his face. His little brother was getting married and he was best man.

Nita's cousin June and Margaret another cousin, were bridesmaids, both dressed in apple green. Clive, her cousin George's six year old son was a very reluctant pageboy. He was all dressed up in sunflower yellow trousers with a white top and he hated it. He threatened to take the whole lot off and walk up the aisle behind the bride wearing only his socks and pants.

'I won't feed you for days and days if you dare to be so stupid,' warned his mother hysterically.

Pamela, a pretty little five year old bridesmaid was very happy with her dress, her shiny shoes and her curly hair with ribbons in it. She was Nora's daughter, Bruce Barton's niece.

Nita looked as fresh as a spring morning when she walked up the aisle dressed in a white satin and lace dress she had hurriedly designed and made herself. Her father was there to give her away, reluctantly it must be said. He had relented at the last minute, just as Dolly had predicted.

There was just one unexpected hitch to the proceedings. The organist, one of Tony's cousins, sent a telegram to say that unfortunately she would not be able to make it. Telegrams were not read out until the reception so no-one knew why the organist was so very late. In the end they prevailed upon a member of the congregation to fill the gap.

Nita's boss attended the ceremony together with his wife and children. Nita had spent many happy years working for the Deaf and Dumb Institute where he was the superintendent.

An old friend of both the Spencer brothers was there, Bruce Lemonde. They had kept in touch since their first meeting aboard the *Duchess of Atholl* on their way to Canada as war-guests during the war.

Nita's Uncle Sid, and Auntie Ivy, June's parents were there. Peter Barton kept darting about taking photographs so didn't manage to get into the wedding pictures himself. Lily Patterson was there who worked at Fegan's Head Office as a secretary. Ruth Horton, an old school friend was also able to come to see Nita married. She'd been a close friend of

Nita's all through senior school and in the Girls' Life Brigade.

They were married by the Rev. Jones in Finlay Road Baptist Church and the reception was held in the panelled room of Gloucester Cathedral.

Tony's aunts were there of course, that is Aunt Sylvia and Aunt Emily, but his Aunt Gladys had refused to come at the last moment. She had somehow expected Tony to travel all the way up to London and escort her down to Gloucester on his wedding day. Instead one of Tony's friends had been given this onerous task.

'I'm not coming young man,' she said, 'and you can tell my nephew from me that I'm very disappointed with his conduct!' She didn't write to the newlyweds for a whole year.

At last it was over. All the good wishes and the tears and the laughter. Nita went to the ladies' room to change into her going away outfit and then they were transported to the station by one of her uncles and chaperoned by Tony's aunts for the very last time. They stood on the platform waiting for the train and suddenly Nita felt tears stinging her eyes. Her time at home as a young person was over. She was no longer Nita Barton. She was Mrs Anthony Spencer. It felt strange as if she'd become someone else.

'Oh, the poor dear is crying for her Mum!' declared Aunt Sylvia sarcastically. Tony was furious with her. Then Dolly Barton turned up just before the train came in. There were hugs and kisses and mother and daughter shed a few tears.

'There now, you'll be all right dear girl,' she said. 'We'll be seeing each other very soon.'

They got into the carriage and sat down. They had it in mind that they must change for Swanage at Weymouth. The chap sitting opposite said:

'Where you off to then?'

'Swanage,' they replied in unison.

'Swanage is it,' said the stranger. 'This train aint goin' there mate,' and he laughed.'

Tony frowned. It wasn't a laughing matter. 'But we are going to Swanage,' he insisted.

'That's as maybe, but you're on the wrong train whichever way you looks at it. This train's going to Swansea!'

The young couple were horrified and started to collect their hand luggage and cases ready to get off at the next mainline station. Then the stranger gave Tony a dig in the ribs. When he turned round, he winked at Tony and mouthed the explanation, 'wedding couple eh?'

'You've been pulling my leg haven't you?' said Tony.

'Does that mean we're on the right train after all?' enquired Nita.

'I couldn't resist having a little joke with you, seeing that you're just married an' all!' said the prankster before wishing them good luck and goodbye.

The newlyweds arrived at their posh Swanage hotel and that night shyly entered the marriage bed as two young lovers experiencing the mysteries of sex for the very first time. She was a young maiden brought up in an old-fashioned Christian way and never thought of doing anything but wait for her Mr Right to come along and now he had. Tony was a sailor, that was true, but first and foremost in his life was his faith. He had also waited for his ladylove to come along and she had. They were both unashamedly as innocent as their original forbears had been in their God-given Garden and like them they delighted in each other and in their good fortune. After the short honeymoon, Tony returned to HMS *Mercury* and was commissioned to HMS *Duchess* on 21st February having been promoted to leading signalman.

The newlyweds had one more precious night together in a seaside hotel in Southsea before it was time to walk to the War Memorial and have that last lingering goodbye kiss. Then Tony left to join his ship.

'Look,' he said to the skipper as the *Duchess* was leaving Portsmouth Harbour, 'that's my wife on the foreshore!'

'Right,' said the skipper, 'blow the whistle!'

Nita heard it and saw her husband waving as she stood standing by the war memorial all wrapped up against the bitterly cold wind. Tony was handed a scope by one of the officers. He peered through it and found his Nita in her red coat. 'Goodbye dearest,' he whispered, 'goodbye.' And that was the last he saw of her until October.

Wedding 11th Feb 1956

CHAPTER 22

The Darings!

HMS *Duchess* left Portsmouth and arrived in Gibraltar on March 7th. Tony had to go ashore to Gibraltar Signal Station for further training, but was also able to get into a hockey match, winning 3.1. Then it was on to Malta where the crew was put to work sprucing up the ship. Even the signalmen had to scrub down and paint the flag deck.

There were many new crew members on board so that it was important for the whole ship's company to do a 'work up' until everyone was up to scratch in their duties.

Duchess was a daring class destroyer, but of a completely different design to *Saintes* , Tony's last ship. It was bigger and had up to the minute technical equipment. They had been built to replace the battles. In spite of this, Tony took a bit of time settling in. *Saintes'* crew had been such a great bunch, it was no wonder that at the beginning of his posting, he missed his old mates.

Duchess was part of a new flotilla of 'Darings' which included HMS *Diamond*, HMS *Decoy*, HMS *Defender* and HMS *Diana*. They all sailed to Malta in convoy, but *Defender* went on to Suez to carry out patrol duties. Captain Nigel Austin was big brass - a four-ring captain not only of HMS *Duchess,* but also captain in charge of the flotilla. He ran a tight ship, kept the crew on their toes and was well respected by the men.

The crew were worked hard, frequently going out on manoeuvres with their sister ships in the Med. They carried out exercises using their big guns by bombarding a tow and using long metal barges with talls masts for target practice. On the 20th they sailed for Barcelona chasing submarines as an exercise on the way.

'The men on the subs enjoyed outwitting the 'Darings' said Tony. 'They would suddenly surface and shout: 'Hey, over here mates. Missed us again!' When the 'Darings' did manage to locate them, hand grenades were quickly dropped over the side as depth charges before they managed to escape.

The *Duchess* crew got to know the ropes pretty quickly. After the depth charges were dropped, the ship would circle round and go back and pick up, not dead mariners, but lots of lovely fish. The depth charges knocked the fish out and they would float to the surface. The sailors would become fishermen resulting in a super fish supper for all on board.

Tony enjoyed target practice. A target would be constructed using two pieces of wood shaped like a cross with a pole sticking out of it with a flag flying on top of it. The best shot on the ship was the skipper. Firing was carried out using 303 rifles and Bren guns.

On March 22nd, Tony was awarded his good conduct badge. *Duchess* was back in Malta and he was given the forenoon off duty. He had two precious letters from Nita so decided to stay aboard in the mess, reading, remembering and, sharing his off duty with her.

Gradually he got on top of his increasing responsibilities as a leading signalman on the *Duchess*. He teamed up with Harry Tate, another leading signalman in the mess who was about the same age as himself. Harry had a great sense of humour - always a great asset on board ship. He introduced Tony to Ron Humphreys, but as Tony says: 'He was much older than us, at least twenty-five!'

Then he was sent to Riscali, a naval shore base, for more signal exams with a view to promotion. He passed the course and was all set to become a yeoman of signals. While the ship was in dry dock in May, Tony and Harry took the opportunity of visiting the Rabat Catacombs.

They extend for miles under the sea and they soon realised how easy it would be to walk up one of the caves and lose one's sense of direction.

'Don't wander off on your own,' said one of the keepers. We're still looking for some poor devil who went missing four or five months ago. Who knows, you might come across him in your travels!'

They learned from the guide that the Maltese had probably used the catacombs in the distant past as a burial ground. They could well believe it. An all enveloping sense of heaviness seemed to descend upon them as they wandered in and out of the huge dark caves ensuring that they kept close to tried and tested pathways.

For centuries the caves had been frequented by smugglers and some Maltese still believed that they harboured hoards of buried treasure. Tony and Harry kept their eyes peeled for any sign that might indicate that they were near these hoards, but had no luck.

'That was a breeze,' said Harry with a laugh when they had finished the tour. The navy lads had seen quite a few human bones scattered about, but found no evidence of the smugglers buried treasure.

'Perhaps the bones were the remains of treasure hunters who wouldn't give up the search,' said Tony. 'A timely warning to us all!' said Harry.

Duchess sailed from Malta on June 2nd for Instanbul. Tony and some of the lads were soon able to leave the ship and explore the Turkish capital. Some of the men preferred to go on a drinking spree hoping to find some exotic belly dancers, but Tony, Harry and another couple of signalmen being interested in history decided to explore the city.

In their search for interesting places to visit they were guided to the famous Blue Mosque. They found it to be as beautiful as they had been led to believe. It was constructed almost entirely of blue marble. Tony had never seen anything quite like it.

The Turkish guide who showed the navy men around spoke very good English. He stopped in what looked like a bay. The marble slabs in the bay were huge. 'A big marble slab was split straight down the middle in the quarry,' he said, 'producing the two slabs you see here. If you look closely you'll see something strange.' The men took a closer look. 'The first panel on the right has the face of the devil right in the middle of it.' The navy lads could plainly see the face of the devil grinning at them malevolently. 'The other panel has the image of a cross in the centre,' said the guide.

The sailors were surprised to seen an image of the Christian cross in a marble slab in a mosque. They wondered what it could mean and looked to the guide expecting some sort of explanation. But he just shrugged his shoulders.

'I do not know what to say about this,' he said. 'I can only say that I feel there is a mystery here.' Then he walked away. The tour was over.

Tony was mystified by this experience. Was it significant, he wondered or just some superstitious accident of nature? He couldn't be sure. Certainly both Muslim and Christians believed in an evil power known as 'the devil', but they differed about the significance of the 'cross'. He had respect for all faiths, but whether the images in the marble were real or imaginary, his allegiance was to Christ and no devil was ever going to change that!

Duchess sailed for Cyprus in June and anchored in Karaovisski Bay. They were there on patrol duty. The Greek Cypriots and Turkish Cypriots both reckoned they should hold sovereignty over the island. The British, who had military bases on Cyprus, endeavoured to keep the warring factions apart, but were sometimes the casualty caught in the middle.

It was the job of British navy destroyers to prevent gun-running. They would hale large fishing vessels and if they volunteered information about the nature of their business and destination would for the most part be allowed to proceed, but sometimes there would be a hostile reaction.

On one such occasion, Tony was signalman of the boarding party. He had been chosen, not only because he was a leading signalman, but also because he held a current marksman's certificate. Like the officer in charge, he was armed with a pistol and he wasn't afraid to use if, should it prove to be necessary. The other seamen in the whaler carried rifles and one a sub-machine gun. This was a deadly serious business.

'Who is the captain of this vessel? 'demanded the officer in charge of the boarding party. There was no reply from the Turkish crew, only a menacing bunching together intended to intimidate the British naval patrol. Brandishing their weapons, the boarding party insisted on being shown over the boat. The crew were obstructive. When some long wooden locked packing cases were discovered, they refused to open them for inspection.

'Send a signal to *Duchess,* Spencer, that we'll be taking this fishing boat in tow,' said the officer. The crew knew then that the game was up. One of them became really nasty and shouted to his compatriots to disarm the sailors and throw them overboard.

'Don't be so stupid,' shouted the naval officer. Look out to sea. Our destroyer has big guns trained upon your vessel. You don't stand a chance!'

They were beaten for the time being, but remained sullen and defiant. It was clear that they would continue the fight for their cause despite the presence of the British Royal Navy.

Their objective was to get guns from Turkey into Cyprus to be used against the Greeks and the British if they got in their way. The Greeks were also involved in smuggling arms from Greece to be used against the Turks. But to the seamen, it made no odds. Whoever was gun-running had to be stopped. Law and order on the island of Cyprus had to be maintained or there would be terrible bloodshed between the opposing ethnic groups in their struggle to gain supremacy.

There was another occasion when it was touch and go. Tony was on a patrol with his ship's captain which involved travelling in a Land Rover from Famagusta to Nicosia. In front of their Land Rover was another carrying some war correspondents and a cameraman. Captain Austin was due to attend a top brass military conference on the island.

Suddenly all hell broke loose. The Land Rover carrying the journalists was blown sky high. Capt. Austin shouted to his driver, 'Get out of here. Now!' The driver swerved, put his foot down, and they were propelled ahead at break neck speed. Later when they were out of harm's way, Tony said to no-one in particular, 'That was a close shave! For a moment there I wondered if we were going to make it!' Captain Austin just grinned and patted his driver on the back. Tony remembers how cool and level-headed he had been under fire.

That summer of '56 was an exceptionally hot one. But nonetheless it was 'action stations' all the time. Day and night they had to be on their mettle, alert, ready for anything. By the end of their six weeks tour of duty, the crew were decidedly jumpy and more than ready to be sailing back to Malta for re-provisioning, ship repairs and a well earned spot of leave.

Once back in Malta, Tony popped in to the Floriana club to meet up with some mates. He was more than surprised to bump into Ray Smith. He hadn't seen or heard of him since their training days together at HMS *Ganges* - all of five years ago.

'Well,' said Tony, 'fancy meeting you here. What have you been up to?'

'I've been having a whale of a time serving as a sparker on board ship, but I found myself a lovely girl and got hitched,' said Ray. 'I'm shore based now at the signal station on Lascaris. What about yourself?'

Tony told Ray a bit about his time on *Cadiz* and *Saintes* and most importantly that he was also a married man.

'Well then, said Ray, 'why don't you get your wife out here Tony, and have a two year shore-based posting on Lascaris? If your wife is anything like my good lady, she'll love it out here!'

It sounded just the ticket to Tony. He went back on board *Duchess* that very day and put in a request for a transfer to Lascaris . He told his senior officer that now that he was married he wanted his wife to join him in Malta and this was the main reason he wanted to be shore-based. This started the ball rolling, but he knew that it would take some time for his application to come up before the 'powers that be' for consideration .

In September he was still impatiently waiting for good news regarding his transfer application when he suddenly decided, come what may, he was going to have his wife with him in Malta.

He sent not one telegram, but many to Nita who was still living at home with her parents informing her that he was getting a flat ready and to quickly make arrangements to fly out and join him a.s.a.p. True to his word, he quickly found a beautiful flat at a place called Marsa - Princess Elizabeth Buildings in Balby Street. This was really due to the good offices of his friends, Ray and Pauline Smith and a Welsh airman, known to all his friends as 'Taff' and his wife.

Nita remembers that time vividly. 'Mum and Dad didn't really want me to go out to Malta. I'd only ever been out of the country once on holiday to Jersey,' she said, 'and I'd never been up in plane. Just the thought of flying out to Malta on my own, was enough to give me the collywobbles, but my family knew and I knew that I had to join my husband. I just had to grit my teeth and get on with it!'

But the journey was to prove horrendous. It was a small plane which seemed unable to withstand much of the turbulence of the wind which resulted in it being tossed up and down like a yo-yo. Nita was sick into little brown bags more times than she thought was possible with nothing in her stomach. Her fears were not allayed when the plane had to make not one but two unscheduled landings because of engine trouble.

'We knew that there was some fighting out in the Mediterranean,' said Nita, 'and all of the passengers felt extremely uneasy.'

Nita flew into Malta on October 27th. In the end it was the Welsh airman 'Taff' who took Tony to Lucca airport to meet her. The plane was four hours late!

'Nita came off the plane, looking like a ghost,' recalls Tony. We took her straight back to the flat in Taff's car. I was expecting her to be over the moon about it. It was such a smashing flat, but even though she was pleased to see me, she was so traumatized by the awful journey, that I had to put her to bed and wait for the next day for her to break out with the 'Oohs and Ahs!'

At last the young couple were reunited. Tony took his young wife sight-seeing and then he proudly introduced her to his friends at the Floriana Club in Valetta. On the Sunday of their first week-end together they attended the Methodist church in the company of Mr and Mrs Reynolds. Horace Reynolds was a senior official responsible for the dockyard. They were a very hospitable couple and always ready to befriend young servicemen away from home.

Tony had gleefully anticipated a whole week of leave to spend with Nita, but he and Nita were in for a nasty shock. He went back on board *Duchess* and wasn't even allowed to get a message through to Nita to let her know that his ship would be sailing for Suez the following morning.

But he did manage to get a message through to Ray Smith who was a telegraphist at the Navy Signals base in Lascaris. Immediately Ray saw the details he smiled wryly and shook his head.

'*Duchess* is away. Poor old Nita!'

There was nothing Tony could do about it.

His diary for that time reads: 'Nita arrived on October 27th. *Duchess* sailed for Cyprus October 29th. Whatever is my dear wife going to make of this?'

Third Ship - HMS Duchess

CHAPTER 23

Not the Best of Times

Nita Spencer was devastated by the news that Tony had been spirited away to God knew where when she had only just come to be with him in Malta. She was a shy, quiet young woman at the best of times and this was definitely not the best of times. She wondered what on earth she would find to do with herself, all alone in a strange country bereft of husband, family and friends.

Ray and Pauline Smith came to her rescue. Ray had a week's leave and they included Nita in their outings to places of interest. But she did have to cook for herself. She was under the impression that she was not allowed to avail herself of the NAAFI facilities for servicemen and their wives because the Navy had not arranged for her to join her husband in Malta.

One day she ventured out on her own to explore the shops of Valetta. The money was similar - she was thankful for that, Maltese pounds, shillings and pence. She found the market place and was able to buy fruit and vegetables. But it wasn't much fun doing this on her own. She had imagined doing it together with Tony, at least for the first week when she had expected him to be on leave. She really enjoyed cooking and had looked forward to preparing delicious meals and watching her husband delighting in whatever she managed to place before him.

She was a young woman of twenty-two and living abroad and away from home for the first time. In the early fifties there was still no television, no telephone in her flat, not even a radio. When she was alone in the evenings she was reduced to knitting, writing letters home as well as to Tony and relying on Tony's friends in Malta to give her a bit of company. Mr and Mrs Reynolds were very good in this respect. She would attend the Methodist church in Floriana and they would invariably invite her back for Sunday lunch.

There was no knowing when Tony would be returning. Nita says that she got so low in spirits in the first two or three weeks that she would definitely have flown back home to England if she hadn't had such an awful journey getting out to Malta. It was all too fresh in her mind. It would take a lot to get her airborne again.

In the meantime, Tony was like a bear with a sore head. Harry Tate couldn't get a civil word out of him. He'd gone to a lot of trouble to get his wife out to Malta. Since they'd been married they'd had little or no time together. He thought that the least the navy could have done was to give him a week's leave when she landed on the rotten island.

However, even though he didn't like it, he had to lump it. On the morning of October 29th they were bound for Suez with their sister destroyers, HMS *Diana, Diamond* and *Decoy.* By the 30th Tony couldn't help noticing that the whole of the British Navy seemed to be sailing full speed ahead for Suez as well. No-one seemed to know what was going on, but the crew sensed that something was up.

'What's going on Tony?' asked Harry. 'There seems to be an awful lot of us going to Cyprus?'

'I don't know,' said Tony, 'but whatever's up it's got to be pretty big, that's for sure!'

In his diary he noted: 'Weather good. October 31st, course and full speed continuing. I still have a strong feeling that this is much more than just a routine exercise.'

The ships were practising, 'action stations' and were put through their paces at all hours of the day and night. By November 1st, Tony's diary records: 'The balloon has gone up! We're bound for Suez!'

They were issued with lifebelts and even closed up at 'action stations' i.e., sleeping with one eye open, ready for any emergency. Then the captain broadcast to the ship's company about the gravity of the situation in Suez. 'Men, the situation in Suez has deteriorated. The navy is needed to support our troops stationed in the Canal. Our objective is to keep the Canal open for international shipping. I have been working you hard and not without good reason. All our efforts as a destroyer in Her Majesty's navy have been to prepare us for such a time as this. We are ready. You all know what you have to do. Stay calm. Stay focused. Do a good job and everyone back home will be proud of what you do today!'

In Tony's case his duty was to serve the officers, to carry incoming signals to the officers and to send signals from time to time to other ships in the fleet.

Then the air strikes started. The French aircraft carrier *Layfayette* and the English carrier, *Ark Royal* were sending off planes to strike fuel dumps in Egypt, just south of Port Said.

'There were about eighty thousand British soldiers out there,' said Tony 'and Nasser was spoiling for a fight. They needed all the help they could get!'

The crew of HMS *Duchess* was put on full-alert during the first watch 6 - 12 hours and saw action from torpedo motor boats, but was not hit. It was scary for the crew, but they were a determined bunch and ready for anything Nasser and his Egyptian forces could throw at them.

Most of the ship's company were young sailors in their early twenties and quite a few still in their teens. They had never been on 'active' service. Suddenly they realised that they were going to war. The complement of men was two hundred and twenty, including the officers who gave the ratings enormous support even though many of them had never been under fire themselves.

About a mile off shore were stationed two or three aircraft carriers and about thirty destroyers. *Duchess* was not in the Canal, but standing off in the Med opposite to Port Said. Signals were received by light or semaphore and sent out in the same way.

Tony would receive a signal, another signalman would write it down, then it would be taken to the first lieutenant, then to the navigation officer and so on to the captain. This was all carried out at top speed. Sometimes an emergency signal would come in in plain language and would be taken immediately to the captain.

It was a traumatic time. Things were volatile, changing rapidly. *Duchess* bombarded the shore with her big guns. All along the shore were beach huts. *Duchess* trained her guns, opened fire and the beach huts were blown to kingdom come. They were there to display their power to do serious damage and to leave the Egyptian forces in no doubt that the British Navy and the French Navy for that matter, were deadly serious. They would do whatever they had to do to secure their objective.

The next day they approached the beach at 04.00 hours and opened up with the big guns. There was havoc - fires breaking out all over the place. It was a nasty moment for the *Duchess* and her crew, but they knew it would be much worse for those ashore.

The day after they went out from anchorage to patrol, they had an emergency on board. A crew member had to be transferred in the middle of all the mayhem, to one of the carriers, suffering from acute appendicitis. Then Tony received the signal that *Duchess* was to be relieved from patrol duty by *Barfleur*.

Duchess weighed anchor and in convoy with *Decoy* set sail for Malta on November 9th. She needed to re-provision and to go into dry dock for essential repairs. The vibrations produced by sailing at top-speed on her way out to Suez had caused structural damage and she was taking in water. The pumps were holding, but it would be foolhardy to wait until they could no longer cope.

Once back in Malta there was very little time for the men to take it easy. The captain was keen to keep his crew on their toes. HMS *Duchess* was sea-worthy and on its way to Limasol in Cyprus by the end of November to relieve two other ships. The ships on duty in Suez were holding their own, but the navy still had Cyprus to sort out.

Tony's diary notes: 'On the 29th Cyprus 0600 hrs. Relieved HMS

Wizard on patrol. Did not sail from Cyprus until 1600 hrs. *Wizard* and *Wakeful,* both frigates, left at 1400 hrs. No mail!'

Duchess went back to Port Said in December. She was expecting to pick up a walking army officer by the name of Moorhouse who had gone ashore to negotiate some sort of peace treaty. He was killed while ashore, some said, 'murdered!'

It remained a very dangerous area. Tony Spencer and Harry Tate were standing on the flag deck looking out over Port Said when suddenly there was the crack and crackle of gun fire right above their heads. They immediately dropped down behind a canvas screen. Fortunately for them it was painted in the same colour as the ship, so at least gave the semblance of protective cover. They had been spotted as potential easy targets by an Egyptian sniper.

'If he had just lowered his sights, it would have been curtains for us,' said Tony. 'One of our chaps on the bridge got him with a machine gun! We had a good laugh about it when we back into the main signal office, but really it was no laughing matter. We had been that close to being taken out. It sent a shiver up our spines!'

Soon after the *Duchess, Decoy* and *Diamond* received their sailing orders and the crew were thrilled to learn that they would be back in Malta for Christmas.

Meanwhile, back at the navy radio station in Malta, Ray Smith received the signal - *Duchess, Diamond* and *Decoy* returning to Malta on December 25th. Tony Spencer is on *Duchess,* he thought. I'll tell Nita when I see her on Sunday.

'Nita,' he said when they met after the Methodist church service, 'I've got some great news for you. Tony's arriving next Tuesday morning, 8 o'clock.

'But that's Christmas Day,' she said. 'You mean, he's coming home for Christmas?'

'It looks like it,' grinned Ray.

Nita could hardly sleep a wink on Christmas eve and was up with the lark on Christmas morning. Long before 8 o'clock she was up, washed, dressed and out of the flat, down the stairs and on her way walking briskly to Customs House. She wanted to meet Tony as soon as he came in on one of the liberty boats. She joined the excited crowd that had gathered there, but it seemed like an eternity of waiting before the shout went up:

'Here they come. Here they come!'

In the end she was taken by surprise. She had known that *Duchess* was coming in, but had no idea that *Diamond* and *Decoy* would be accompanying her. That made it special, magical. She was momentarily transported back to Gloucester and Christmases spent with her family. Her dear Mum would be seated at the piano and the rest of the family would be standing around singing for all they were worth:

'I saw three ships come sailing in On Christmas Day, on Christmas Day; I saw three ships come sailing in, On Christmas Day in the morning. Sailing into Grand Harbour were three grand ships, HMS Duchess, HMS Decoy and last but not least, HMS Diamond on Christmas Day in the morning.

'I saw about six or seven liberty boats come in,' said Nita, 'but Tony wasn't in any of them. I wondered what had happened to him. Where on earth was he? Perhaps he wasn't in a hurry to get ashore!'

'Where's Tony Spencer?' she asked one of the sailors who had come in off the *Duchess*.

'I expect he got off on the other side,' he said. In the end she decided to walk back to the flat, hoping to find him there.

When *Duchess* came into Grand Harbour to Birkakara, Tony got permission to go ashore immediately because his wife was in Malta. He didn't know that Nita had been expecting him and was waiting for him at Customs House. He walked the short distance to the flat, let himself in and was disappointed to find the flat empty. He noticed that the bed had been slept in, so was sure that Nita must have been there overnight. He was puzzled. Where was she?

There was a knock on the door. It was his RAF mate, Welshman Taff from the upstairs flat.

'Hello there Tony,' he said. 'Good to see you back in one piece boyo! Been having it a bit rough eh?'

'I'm all right,' said Tony, 'but I can't make out where my wife has gone!'

'Ray Smith told Nita your ship would be coming in today. She probably went down to the harbour to meet you. It looks as if you missed each other,' he said laughing.

'So that's it,' said Tony. 'I thought I was going to surprise her, but she knew already!'

'I'll be off now. See you later. Happy Christmas!'

Tony was making himself a cup of tea in the kitchen when he heard Taff calling out to him:

'Your good lady is coming up the stairs, Tony!'

And suddenly, there she was. What a picture, he thought.

'Where the hell have you been?' he said which was not what he meant to say at all.

'Waiting for you to come in up at Customs House,' Where were you anyway?' replied Nita, more than a little hurt by his outburst.

'I'm sorry love. I shouldn't have snapped at you like that. Happy Christmas! Come here and give me a kiss.'

Nita burst into tears. She felt so stupid because she couldn't find her handkerchief.

'You'll never know just how much I missed you, dear. It's wonderful to be home and together again,' he said.

In the days that followed, Tony harassed the divisional officer every day about his transfer, but in the end the officer had to break the disappointing news. 'I'm sorry Spencer, but it's a no-go. *Duchess* was unable to find a relief for you. You've got to stay on board and that's about it mate.'

Nita had been out in Malta for two months, mostly without Tony, but now they had to make preparations for their return home. *Duchess* was due to return to the UK soon after Christmas and Nita knew that like it or not, she would have to take to the skies again.

'Tony's ship sailed a day before Nita's flight. It was so much better than the outward journey that she almost enjoyed it. She had a window seat and looking out at the sea below saw the wake of three ships and knew that one of them was *Duchess* on its way home.

During the journey, she had time to reflect all that had happened since leaving her family to join her sailor husband. She had arrived in Malta a shy, nervous young woman, but she'd had to grow up fast when Tony left Malta to go to Suez. Like the other sailors' wives, she had worried about her man knowing that he was in danger and like them, she had experienced the greatest sense of relief and joy when her husband had returned safely.

She was happy to be going home again to see her Mum and Dad and brothers in Gloucester, but things had changed. She had settled into her new role as married lady and from now on 'home' would always be wherever she and Tony could be together.

CHAPTER 24

Home and Abroad

The *Duchess* sailed from Malta on January 1st 1957. It took three days to get back to England. Even though Tony loved to venture abroad, he was always happy to return to his homeland.

The men were given a spot of leave and Tony made his way up to Gloucester to join Nita. He felt really at home with Nita's family, but knew it was time to look for their own place in Portsmouth. They eventually found a home with Mr and Mrs Clark in Torrington Road. The first floor flat had been beautifully decorated and tastefully furnished, but the young couple hadn't been long in residence before a minor disaster upset the apple cart.

One day, Nita was happily cooking an evening meal for her sailor husband and forgot that she had left a chip pan on a low gas in the kitchen. They had finished their dinner and were thinking about clearing the table when Tony was alarmed to hear SNAP! CRACKLE! and POP! issuing from the direction of the kitchen. He turned his gaze towards it and saw flames leaping from a pan on the gas cooker.

He was on his feet in a flash, flew into the kitchen and did the first thing that came into his head. He grabbed hold of the hot fire-filled pan, dumped it in the kitchen sink and turned the cold tap full on. There was an almighty WHOOSH! and flames shot straight up and hit the ceiling.

Nita rushed in to help, but there was nothing she could do. The kitchen was as black as a chimney sweep and so was Tony! Amazingly the whole of the kitchen was not on fire and no-one had been hurt!

The Clarks were not very happy when they heard what had transpired and saw the extent of the damage. 'Mr Clark took it all right,' said Tony, 'but Mrs Clark became all hot and bothered.'

'How could you be so stupid,' she reprimanded them. 'What on earth were you thinking of! The house could have been burned to the ground!'

'Come on now mother,' said her husband, 'let's not get hysterical.'

'But we've only just finished decorating the flat. Now look at it!'

Tony interrupted her moans and groans by cheerfully offering to set to work immediately to clean up the kitchen walls and ceiling and throw on some more paint. Surprisingly this did not have the desired effect on Mrs Clark. She burst into tears, turned on her heel and left the room quickly followed by her husband.

'What did I say?' said a puzzled Tony to Nita. 'I thought she'd be pleased!'

They couldn't put the matter to rights with Mrs Clark so they did the next best thing. They took off up to Gloucester with their tails between their legs. When they returned a week later wondering what their reception would be, they were shocked to find the flat in pristine condition. They were welcomed as if nothing had happened to spoil the budding relationship with their landlady and the regrettable 'incident' was never mentioned again.

Soon Tony had to return to his duties aboard *Duchess*. A big exercise was about to take place in the Channel and off Ushant towards Ireland which involved the American Fleet and some French ships. For the most part Tony could go on board every day to perform his duties as a leading signalman and return to his married quarters at night.

At last there was time for Nita and Tony to get to know each other and the good people in the local church. Tony was a happy man. He had his own place and his own little wife to come home to. What more could any man want!

One day he arrived home all excited. 'We're off to America, Nita,' he said. 'It's all right for some,' she replied. 'Are the wives invited?' 'No, my sweet, not this time. But I'll take you one day. You'll see!'

Nita was happy for her husband. She was more of a home bird and quite content for Tony to go off gallivanting to foreign parts just so long as she knew that he was safe and would be coming back home to her.

On her way to the States, the *Duchess* was again involved in combined fleet exercises. Half way across the Atlantic she came across a replica of the famous *Mayflower* . They were in convoy with *Ark Royal* and *Diamond* and these mighty ships circled the little sailing vessel. A helicopter hovered above and dipped its nose in salute. All the men thought back to the time when the original *Mayflower* left Plymouth Hoe on September 6th 1620 bound for the New World. In spite of many hazards and loss of life, Captain Jones and many brave men, women and children eventually made it, landing at Cape Cod. The replica - *Mayflower II* is now berthed in Plymouth, Massachusetts.

The convoy from the UK first stopped off in Bermuda. Tony had a bicycle on board and with Reg Wantling took the opportunity to have a look around the beautiful island. It was a Sunday. The weather was marvellous. Blue skies, turquoise seas and tropical sunshine. On the way back to the ship, Tony noticed a little whitewashed clapboard church, built in the old Colonial style. 'I'm going in,' said Tony to his mate. 'See you later.' It was just the right time for the evening service. He joined the locals as they sauntered in.

When he sat down he wondered why there seemed to be a hum from the congregation. All eyes were turned upon him as if he had two heads or something. Then the penny dropped. He was the only white person in the church. All the others were black or coloured. Tony didn't mind and he hoped the church members didn't.

Then the music started up, everyone began clapping and the choir sang out loud and clear, encouraging the congregation to get on their feet and start praising the Lord. So far, so good, thought Tony. He always enjoyed a lively service. But he was taken aback when the tall black Minister stood before the people to lead them in prayer. He recognized him at once. It was none other than Mr Sommerskill. One of the Master's at Fegan's Home for Boys. 'You could have knocked me down with a feather,' said Tony. 'I couldn't believe my eyes.'

Mr Sommerskill couldn't help noticing the stranger in the midst. Tony knew that he had been recognized by the big grin on his face as he looked at him. After the prayers, he informed the congregation:

'Today church, we have a good friend come among us. The good Lord has brought all the way from England a lad I knew many years ago when I was serving Him in Fegan's Boys Home. Let us give a good old-fashioned Bermudan welcome to Anthony Spencer!'

To his embarrassment, the whole congregation stood up and faced him. They clapped and sang their welcome. Some came up to him to shake him by the hand. Others gave him a big bear hug. 'They made me feel like I was one of them,' said Tony 'as if we were all just one big family.'

As soon as the meeting was over, Tony was whisked out of the church and driven to the Rev. Sommerskill's house where he and his wife gave him a hearty meal before escorting him back to his ship. 'They treated me like a long lost son,' he said. 'It was marvellous!'

The convoy sailed on to Norfolk, Virginia in the USA Their objective was to take part in an International Fleet Review. They were due to join up with as many as a hundred or more ships that would be gathering together for the great occasion. But the funny thing is Tony missed it all.

After his ship had been in Norfolk for a couple of days, a Lt. Commander from the American Navy was piped aboard and gave out an invitation to the crew:

'Welcome to the United States of America. If any of you guys has any close connections with folks in North America, the American Navy would be happy to put you in touch with them at this time.'

Immediately Tony thought of his Auntie Lil and Uncle Eli in

Ontario, Canada. He went to his divisional officer and made his request official. After just twenty four hours he was informed that he was the only crew member who had any connections with people in the USA or Canada. His request was granted. Within days he was on his way to the American Air force base in Norfolk.

'Hi there sailor. Where are you off to?' enquired an American naval officer with a big grin on his face.

'I want to go to Toronto, sir,' he said.

'Name of Spencer, leading signalman with the British Navy?' said the officer. 'We've got it all laid on for you! One of our boys is going to Washington. He'll drop you off.'

Tony left in a jet plane en route to Washington DC. The crew were wonderful to him. Treated him like royalty. They probably thought he knew the royal family personally and often visited the palace for high tea and cucumber sandwiches when he was up in town!

'We don't usually have the privilege of flying British navy chaps,' said the pilot. 'It's usually just our own fellas. What do you think of our country so far?'

'Great!' said Tony enthusiastically 'I've never been in a jet before - only a helicopter.'

The pilot was very happy to announce that they were flying over the capital, Washington and to prove it he flew around the White House twice. Tony was suitably impressed. They came into land and he was put on board a Beachcomber.

'Where are you going sailor?' he asked Tony 'To Toronto,' replied Tony. 'Is that so?' he said as if he was surprised. Just for a moment or two Tony wondered if there had been some hiccup in the system and he'd caught the wrong plane.

'Well,' said the pilot with a Southern drawl, 'I'm not allowed to fly over the border. You ring your folks in Canada and get them to meet you in Detroit.'

'Is that you Uncle Eli, it's Anthony. Yes, Anthony Spencer!'

The Lawrences knew that Tony would be coming to America to the International Fleet Review, but they had no idea he would be able to visit them in Canada.

'You'll meet me on the USA side of Niagara Falls? Great. Can't wait to see you both.'

The pilot knew a couple who lived in the UK by the name of Newman and was puzzled when Tony had to confess that he hadn't met them and didn't know them.

'But they live in Norfolk, England,' said the pilot as if Tony must surely know everyone who lived there.

'I've only been there once,' he explained, 'not long enough to get to know any of the local people.'

'But you're country is kinda small isn't it?' the pilot persisted. 'I sort of expected you all to get to be real buddies with everyone pretty quickly!'

'It may seem small to you,' said Tony, 'because America is a big country, 'but there are more than fifty- five million people living there and that's not counting the millions of visitors who come to the UK every year!'

'It was just wonderful to meet Mr and Mrs Lawrence again after so many years,' said Tony. He had kept in touch with them by writing long letters about his adventures and learning about theirs in return. They were living in Aurora, just north of Toronto where they had a smallholding of chickens and strawberry patches.

When he arrived that first night, as soon as they had finished their evening meal, Eli Lawrence said:

'Come on we're off!' They climbed into the big shooting brake and drove 170 miles up north to visit the Larkins who had known the Spencer brothers when they were billeted with the Lawrences during the war. They stayed talking and laughing until the early hours of the morning. Then they made the long journey back home. He was absolutely shattered. It had been a long day. But before hitting the sack, Tony had to renew his friendship with Spot, the dearest dog in the world. She had been his closest companion when he was a boy in Canada. Now she was blind and deaf and very old. 'You poor old girl,' he said as he cuddled and stroked her. 'I never forgot you Spot. You were always my best mate!' She seemed to understand every word.

As soon as his head hit the pillow, he went out like a light. He woke late morning and suddenly remembered where he was. It hadn't been a dream after all. He really was 'back home' in Canada with Uncle Eli and Auntie Lil and his dear old faithful dog, Spot. Then he became aware of her lying close to him underneath the bed clothes. He felt her cold little nose. He uncovered her to give her a greeting, but found that she had died in his bed during the night.

'She couldn't see. She couldn't scamper about any more, but she knew me,' Tony said. 'She had waited for me, hung on until I came back.' In the hall of the Lawrence's bungalow was Spot's basket and underneath her cushion were all of Tony's letters. 'She always got your letters first,' said Lilian Lawrence. 'She used to get so excited even before they came through the letter box. It was as if she knew there'd be a letter from her Anthony!'

'Dear old Spot. I'll never forget her,' Tony said.

All too soon it was time for Tony to return to his ship. Eli Lawrence drove him to Toronto Airport and paid for his flight to Norfolk, Virginia, USA He landed there and got back on board *Duchess* with time to spare.

'And where do you think you've been while we've been slaving away working our fingers to the bone?' said his mess mates.

'How did the Fleet Review go then?' enquired Tony.

'Marvellous!' they said. 'The Americans really know how to give a chap a good time. They're hot on hospitality. We were welcomed into their posh houses with open arms and met some really dishy girls! You see Tony, you missed a great treat!' But Tony knew differently. He wouldn't have missed his Canadian reunion with old friends for the world.

Duchess had to sail up to Newfoundland to fulfil a previously arranged commitment and then it was back across the Atlantic heading for home where Tony was discharged from the *Duchess* and transferred to HMS *Mercury* - a shore base. He was soon to finish the Yeoman's course, qualifying as a 'Yeoman of Signals.'

Another chapter in his life closed when he said goodbye to the *Duchess* and his mess mates. He would miss them. They were all good men and true.

A new life was opening up before him. He was soon to become a father. He wondered if he would measure up to his own high ideal of what a father should be. He'd never known his own father, but he determined to be there for his kids and God helping him, to stick by them and be there for them, come what may.

CHAPTER 25

Arrivals and Departures

Tony nearly missed the birth of his son. He was hospitalized for breathing problems. The doctors discovered a cartilage growth obstructing his sinuses. Surgery was successfully carried out, but post- operatively he contracted a chest infection and was treated with penicillin. He became agitated over his prolonged stay in hospital as Nita's expected delivery date drew near. He was desperate to be with his wife when she went into labour. He badgered the medics from morning till night, insisting that nothing and no-one would prevent him from being present at the birth of his first child. Reluctantly, they agreed to let him go.

Phillip Anthony Spencer was born on October 17th, 1957. He weighed in at 7 lbs 4 ozs. He had a mass of dark hair and cornflower blue eyes. He was perfect. Dolly Barton took great care of her only daughter when she was in labour while her father was pacing the floor downstairs. The baby was delivered by the Barton's long-time family doctor, Dr. Mitchell. Phillip took his time coming, it must be said, but there was great relief and joy apparent on Tony Spencer's face as he cradled his scrawny baby son in his arms. He had made it. He had been there for Nita, rubbing her back, laughing and crying with her all through the long night.

Dolly Barton remembered giving birth to her daughter in her own mother's house in Gloucester many moons ago, but it seemed like yesterday to her. She left Nita, Tony and the baby to go down stairs to break the good news to Bruce Barton, Nita's father. 'It's a boy, Dad!'

'Well I never,' said Bruce Barton as if he could hardly believe it. 'Is she all right then, our Nita?'

'Yes love, she's fine.'

'Shall I go up and see her and the little 'un?'

'Just give them a little time on their own. It's a wonderful thing having your first baby. Don't you remember, Dad?'

'Course I do, old girl. I can't believe my little girl has had to go through all of that! But she's got her own little'un now, and they're both well, thank the Lord!' He took out an enormous white handkerchief, blew his nose loudly and had a discreet dab at his eyes.

Nita was well and so was the baby, but Tony was still not out of the woods. He had noticed when he was rubbing Nita's back that he had blisters on his arms, the backs of his hands and by the time the baby had arrived, all over his body. He was very hot and his head was thumping as if he'd been in a twelve-round fight with the heavy weight champion, Joe Louis. As soon as Dr Mitchell was sure that mother and baby were all right, he turned his attention to the baby's father.

'Tony, you look awful,' he said. 'What's the matter?'

'I don't know,' said Tony, 'but I've got some enormous blisters on my arms and legs, even on my feet.'

The doc looked at the blisters, took Tony's temperature which registered 103F and said, 'I'm not sure what's the matter with you Tony, but you're definitely going down with something. There's an army camp nearby. Get your things together and I'll take you down there for the Army medics to look you over. Nita and the baby will be well looked after here.'

'What's the matter with Tony, doctor?' enquired Nita anxiously when she heard that he had to see an Army doctor straight away.

'I don't know, Nita,' said Dr Mitchell, 'but the best thing is for him to be seen as soon as possible. Now don't you worry yourself. You just look after little Phillip and we'll soon sort his father out!'

Tony was hospitalised once again, but it was a week or two before the doctors realised that he was suffering from a bad case of reaction to the big doses of penicillin he had been given following his chest infection. It took some time before they could get his condition under control, then he was transferred to the naval hospital in Portsmouth, but not without being given strict instructions never to take penicillin again. 'You've had a nasty reaction to it,' said his doctor. 'You've been lucky, but next time, it could be curtains!'

It wasn't until the end of February 1958 that Tony, Nita and the baby were able to return to their flat in Torrington Road, Portsmouth. Tony was fit at last and eager to get back to his duties as a signalman at HMS *Mercury* cycling the seven miles to East Meon there and back every day just to prove he was back to normal. He was put in charge of Visual Signal Stores and given the task of instructing new entrants. Everything was hunky-dory!'

Sometime during the summer months, Dolly Barton wrote to say that Mrs Coleman, an old frail lady in her nineties, who lived next door at No.15 Reservoir Road, was looking to let out some rooms in her house rent free. Her relatives wanted her to have someone in the house at night, to keep an eye on her. Dolly Barton looked in on the old lady every day, did her shopping and kept the place tidy. Nita's Mum was wondering if Nita, Tony and her grandchild would like to come back up to Gloucester and live next door. She was missing her daughter and her grandchild badly and this seemed like a wonderful opportunity for having them close by.

'I've had a letter from Mum,' said Nita to Tony one evening as they sat eating their supper.

'Everything all right?' enquired Tony.

'Yes, but...'

Tony put down his knife and fork and looked at his wife. Something must be up. 'Everything's not all right then?'

'It isn't that,' said Nita. 'Oh, here's the letter. If you read it, you'll know what I'm thinking.'

Tony read the letter. 'So, you'd like to go back up to Gloucester and live next door to your Mum, Nita?'

'Yes, but what do you think Tony? Do you think we should?'

'Well, to tell you the truth, I've been thinking about leaving the navy. My contract of active service and five years reserve is due to end next February. I'm not sure what to do. Should I stay in and renew my contract or leave?'

'Well dear, it's up to you,' said Nita. 'I can't tell you what to do. You love the navy life. I can't imagine you doing anything else, but sooner or later you'll have to go away to sea again for a couple of years and it would be lovely for me and the baby if we were living next door to Mum and Dad.'

'Write to your mum and say we'll be coming to stay in a couple of weeks. Tell her I'll think about Mrs Coleman's accommodation and let her know when we come up.'

In the following weeks Tony brooded over his future. Yes, he loved the navy and didn't want to leave, but he wanted to settle down and be the man about the house for his wife and family. By the time they arrived in Gloucester, he determined to get his wife and baby installed in Mrs Coleman's house and look around the area to see what jobs could be had for an ex. navy signalman.

He found an advertisement in the local paper for a trainee sign writer and told Nita that he'd try for an interview. 'It appeals to me Nita,' he said. 'I'm sure it would be well paid once I was properly trained.'

Tony attended the interview and was offered the job, making sure to tell his future boss that he wasn't due to get out of the navy until February of 1959.

'You're a navy lad and I'd like to give you a chance to better yourself in Civvy Street,' said Mr Cartridge. But the wage was only three pounds per week.

'Three pounds a week!' said Tony aghast. 'I'd like the job, but I couldn't provide for a wife and child on that!'

'Well, we can't offer you more,' said Mr Cartridge. 'You'd have to learn the trade before you could be in any way useful and that takes time. Most chaps would jump at a chance like this!'

It was true. Tony knew it, but he'd have to find something else.

Tony, Nita and Dolly Barton attended the local Baptist church and Dolly let it be known that her son-in-law was thinking of leaving the navy and was looking for a job locally. One of the deacons worked for a big shoe retailer called, *BARRATTS*. He said that they were always looking for prospective trainee managers and once he'd left the navy, an opportunity might present itself, if he would apply. The wages would be in the region of six pounds per week, plus commission.

It wasn't the most exciting job in the world, thought Tony, working in a shoe shop. He was used to big ships, rough seas, wide open spaces with only the sky as a roof over his head, not to mention the camaraderie of ship mates, but it was a job with a secure future and he had to give it serious consideration.

In the meantime, he gave up the flat in Torrington Road and boarded with the other single sailors at HMS *Mercury* getting away to be with Nita and his baby son most week-ends.

He decided that it was time to pay a visit to his aunts in London. He hadn't seen his Aunt Gladys for ages and it was her he had to thank for getting him into the navy in the first place when he was just a lad. He felt he owed it to her to let her know his plans.

'You mean to stand there and tell me that you're thinking of leaving the navy,' said Gladys Butler angrily.

'Yes,' said Tony unabashed. 'If I stay in, I'll have to leave Nita and the baby for years at a time when I go to sea. I don't want that. I want to settle down. I grew up without a mother and a father in an orphanage. I'm going to be there for my wife and family - day in and day out. Anyone can have kids, it's being there for them until they grow up, that's the hard part!'

'I suppose by that you're implying that your Aunt Sylvia and I were never there for you,' said his aunt, very hurt and offended. 'We always did what we considered to be the very best for you and your brother, Anthony, but you never appreciated anything we did,' and she had to fight to hold back her tears.

'No. I'm not blaming you for anything Aunt Gladys,' said Tony. 'I know you did your best for us and I'll always be grateful that you took us to Canada.'

'I suppose it's your wife that's put you up to this. She wants you to leave the navy when it's been the making of you Anthony,' she said bitterly.

'My wife hasn't done anything of the sort,' said Tony. 'You don't know what a dear she is. I'd be nothing without Nita behind me. She's made it clear that its up to me. I'm to do what I want and I want to leave the navy and settle down.'

'Then more fool you!' said his aunt. 'You were always the obstinate one, Anthony,' she said. 'Your brother Godfrey was always more sensible. Look how well he's doing. He married a very nice young lady. He always said he'd have his own business one day and he's already making plans to leave Hiscock & Appleby to set up on his own. I must say, your Aunt Sylvia and I are very proud of him. You disappoint Anthony, but you'll do what you want no matter what we say!'

It seemed to Tony that they had been here before. Godfrey was the clever one and he was the duffer. Godfrey could do no wrong and he could do no right. Godfrey had married a posh bank manager's daughter and he had married a country girl. But he couldn't stay in the navy just to curry favour with his aunts. He knew he would never have the place in their affections that Godfrey had. He would have to do what he knew was the right thing for him and his family and that was that.

When he left the navy on February 8th 1959, he was given a suit, an overcoat, shoes, a small suitcase and enough money to last him and his family for a week, then he was catapulted into civilian life working 8.30 am - 6.00 pm Monday to Saturday with a half day on Wednesday in a shoe shop in Gloucester.

At first he wondered if he could really do this day in and day out for the rest of his life. He didn't know, but he was going to give it his best shot. He was a family man now - a husband and a father. He reminded himself that he wasn't doing it to please himself. He was doing it for them and for them he was determined to be the best shoe salesman the world had ever seen!

CHAPTER 26

Brothers

When Godfrey Spencer left Fegan's Home for Boys, he was transferred to the Farm at Gourdhurst. He was a misfit there and the staff at the Farm knew it. There happened to be a vacancy for an office boy in the head office at Millbank, London. Godfrey was offered the job and was happy to accept it.

He was a bright lad, personable, accommodating and ambitious. He got on well with his Aunt Gladys who offered him a home and he got on well with the young ladies in the office who taught him all he needed to know about office work. After a couple of years, he figured that he was ready to move on. He didn't have to move far. Hiscock and Appleby had their offices upstairs in the same building. They had noticed Godfrey, made enquiries and soon he had a job in their sales department. It was more money and his new bosses were happy to teach him about the big world of commerce. He was on his way.

He was called up in 1950 to do his national service in the Royal Air Force. It was a bit of an interruption to his well laid plans, but he worked in the Record Dept, when on duty and was handsome and charming enough to set many a young WAAF girl's heart a flutter when he wasn't.

When they were young, Godfrey and his younger brother Anthony had always argued and fought, but in spite of their differences there remained a strong bond between them. They had been through the mill together. Godfrey was only a few years older than his 'little' brother, but he was more street-wise and he knew it. When Anthony was transferred to Fegan's farm, he wondered how he would get on. He had hated it, but he reckoned that the big outdoor life, looking after the farm animals and all that sort of thing might appeal to his brother. He was more than a bit surprised when his Aunt Gladys told him that Anthony had written to say that he wasn't at all happy at the farm and wanted to leave as soon as it could be arranged.

'But what will he do, Godfrey?' said Gladys Butler. 'Where will he go?'

'Why can't he come here Aunt?' said Godfrey. 'He can share my room. We'll manage!'

'It's out of the question,' said his aunt. 'You and your brother are quite different, Godfrey. You are sensible, capable. Anthony will never be able to get on like you've done. He never did well at school. He doesn't like farming. What is he able to do - what can he do, Godfrey? I don't want him hanging about the place all day and night!'

'That's a bit unfair aunt, said Godfrey. 'He's a good chap. Give him a chance to think about it and look around. He'll find something.'

'I hope you're right,' said his aunt with a sigh. Her sister's boys were such a weight on her and her sister Sylvia. Godfrey was turning out all right, but what on earth were they to do with Anthony!

There was relief all round when Anthony finally decided that he wanted to go into the navy. Aunt Gladys was on her metal. She moved mountains to see that he got in. Another big problem was solved. Anthony had the opportunity of a good career in the navy with board and lodging provided. Then Godfrey left home to do his National Service. He was sorely missed. The aunts found him easy to have around. He was quiet, bookish. He knew where he was going, what he wanted out of life and went for it.

Godfrey was posted to RAF Records in Gloucester where his future sister-in-law, Nita Barton lived. He even attended Trinity Baptist Church where she was a church member. Things might have turned out very differently if he had met up with Nita and asked her out instead of her best friend, but it was only a fleeting romance.

In 1955 he married June Winser. She came from London. After he left the R.A.F. he had gone back to living with Aunt Gladys and working for Hiscock and Appleby who were into the soft furnishing business. His younger brother was his best man. It was a posh affair. The Winsers were strictly a 'top-hat and tails' family.

Bruce Lemonde - whose mother had befriended Aunt Gladys en route to Canada and had remained a firm friend, was invited to Godrey's wedding and turned up looking very dashing in his naval officer's uniform. It proved to be a happy event for him as well as Godfrey. He met his future wife Peggy at the wedding. She was one of the bridesmaids.

The roles were reversed in 1956 when Anthony married Nita Barton. Godfrey was his best man. There were lots of friends and family on that occasion too, but it was less formal. Anthony and Nita had decided to get married before he went to sea for another two and a half years term of service.

The brothers kept in regular contact. Tony and Nita attended the christening of his brother's son, Gerald and June and Godfrey came to Portsmouth for the dedication of Phillip Anthony Spencer, their first-born.

The brothers even made plans to take a holiday together with their families in the summer of '58, but their plans didn't go down too well with their wives. Godfrey's wife, June had a toddler and was expecting their second child and Nita's Phillip was still only a baby. Godfrey was very annoyed by their objections, but told his brother that the proposed holiday would still take place.

Tony became concerned when after two then three months his brother didn't contact him. He had written, rang him at his offce, left messages, but he didn't get back to him.

'What on earth is he playing at?' he said to Nita one evening. 'This isn't like Godfrey. He must be in some kind of trouble, but why hasn't he let me know!'

'Oh, he's all right. He's just busy, I expect,' said Nita. But Tony wasn't reassured.

Then one day, out of the blue, Godfrey phoned.

'It's over,' he said. 'We've parted. I've left June and got myself a flat.'

'You've what!' said Tony unable to believe what he had just heard. 'You've left your wife, but what about your boys? You can't be serious. After all we went through, you mean to tell me that you're going to put your kids through that!'

'You've got it all wrong, Anthony. I never was into the 'family' thing. Women tie us down with mortgages and their insatiable demands. Then it's always the kids, the kids. I'm sick of it. I can't live my life like that. I'm free now; to go where I want and do what I want and I'm streets better off!'

Tony was mortified. 'I thought we were close. You never let on, you never told me, Godfrey!'

'Oh, you're such a stick in the mud,' said his brother. 'I knew you'd be up the wall about it. Why don't you come and see me. I've taken a flat in London. I'm feeling as rotten as hell and I'm stony broke!'

Tony Spencer was shattered. There was nothing more sacred to him than his faith and 'family'. Godfrey was his family and so were Godfrey's boys. He was desperate to get up to London to see his brother as soon as possible. Perhaps there was still time to salvage the situation. It looked to him as if history was repeating itself. His father had left his mother with a toddler and a baby on the way with devastating results for him and Godfrey. He couldn't let that happen to Godfrey's two boys, Gerald and Julian.

He made the trip up to London the very next day. Godfrey was living in a private block of flats in Kensington Gardens. It was obvious that he'd been drinking and was feeling very sorry for himself.

'Thanks for coming old chap. I'm in a bit of a mess as you can see. Not used to doing my own chores.'

Tony looked around. Godfrey may have been a sharp dresser he thought, but he had no idea how to wash-up or make his bed. The place was littered with empty gin bottles and full ash trays.

'I should lay off the booze, Godfrey,' said Tony. 'We both know that won't solve anything.'

'Just because you've taken the pledge little brother, it doesn't mean we all have to join a monastery!' said Godfrey.

'How can you afford this place?' queried Tony, 'it must cost the earth!'

'I can't afford it and I'm broke. Could you be a good mate and lend me some money Anthony? As soon as I get back on my feet I'll pay you back.'

'Nita and I haven't got much, Godfrey, you know that,' said Tony. 'We have a hard time just making ends meet and Nita's expecting another baby!'

'I know, I know,' said Godfrey, 'but you must have a bit put by for a rainy day. This is it. I'm scraping the bottom of the barrel. You've got to help me out. The aunts think their Godfrey is wonderful and all that nonsense. I can't ask them!'

Godfrey could always twist Tony around his little finger. 'Blood is thicker than water,' he would say. 'You're the only real family I've ever had in this world. We're brothers for God's sake!'

After leaving his brother, Tony made his way across London to see his Aunt Gladys. Something just had to be done about Godfrey. He couldn't leave him like that.

'Anthony,' said Gladys Butler more than surprised to see her nephew. 'Whatever's the matter? You always let us know when you're coming to visit.'

'I've just been to see Godfrey,' said Tony. 'He's in an awful mess. He's broken up from his wife.'

'Well,' said his aunt indignantly. 'What do you expect me or your Aunt Sylvia to do about it? We've always done our best for you both.

But this is beyond us. We never expected Godfrey to let us down like this!'

Tony could see that a couple of old maiden aunts were not the best people in the world to help Godfrey at this point in time. Marriage problems were not their thing.

'I must have my father's address Aunt Gladys,' said Tony. 'I've been trying to get it out of you for years. You've always refused to tell me where he lives, but this time I'm not taking 'no' for an answer. He may be able to talk some sense into Godfrey.'

'That is extremely unlikely,' said Gladys Butler. 'He was always a bad sort. He left your mother with two young children to bring up on her own. Is this the sort of man who'd be able to help Godfrey! He's no good, never was and never will be!'

'That's enough, Aunt Gladys!' said Tony sharply. 'Whatever he did, he's my father. He's the only father I've got and I want to meet him. You had better realise that I'm no longer a little kid you can order around. I'm a married man and a father myself. I insist that you tell me where I can reach him!'

Gladys Butler rose up and left the room shutting the door firmly behind her. Tony wondered if he'd managed to convince her that he meant what he said. She was a hard-nosed woman when crossed. How was she going to cope with his insistence. He could only wait for her to return to find out. He was sure about one thing. He was not going to leave the house that night without his father's address.

She returned, white-faced, tight-lipped and without a word handed him a piece of paper. He looked down and read:

'Mr Peter Spencer
375 Baker Street,
Enfield.'

'I can hardly believe it,' he said aloud. 'I've had to wait all these years for this.'

He looked at his aunt. The hatred and bitterness in her eyes was frightening to see. 'You've got what you want. Now you'd better go,' she said.

It was a bitterly cold winter night, but Tony felt warm inside. He had done what he had to do. It had been painful for him as well as his aunt. He loved her, but he also felt sorry for her. She had let her bitterness against his father fester all these years. No good had come of it.

In the days that followed he took great delight in helping Nita put up the decorations in their new flat in Wiltshire. They had recently moved from Reservoir Road in Gloucester, because Mrs. Coleman, their ailing landlady had died and her relatives had wanted to sell the house. Tony had been very lucky to have found a place in Box not far from Bristol where he worked.

They had a big Christmas tree and Tony lifted his little boy up to fix a star to the top most branch. 'That's the last of the Christmas cards done,' said Nita. 'I hope we haven't forgotten anybody.'

'There's just one more, dear,' said Tony. 'I'm going to send a card to my Dad.'

'Do you think so,' said Nita doubtfully. 'Perhaps you'd better write him a letter to explain things.'

'No, I'll just put a few words on this Christmas card telling him that I'm his son, Anthony and that I'd like him to get in touch with me to discuss some family matters. We'll see what comes of it.'

'If you're sure that's the way to do it,' said Nita. 'He'll probably get lots of cards. It seems a strange way of introducing yourself to your father.'

But almost by return of post, the longed for reply arrived in the form of a letter postmarked, 'Enfield'. 'This is it,' said Tony. 'Perhaps he doesn't want anything to do with us. Perhaps he's replying just to be polite, but wants no further contact.'

'You'll never know if you don't open it,' said Nita.

'Thank you for your Christmas card, Anthony,' he read. *'Evelyn and I would love to meet you. Of course I've told my wife about you and Godfrey. I shall be coming to Bristol on business in the New Year and shall see you then. We wish you, your wife and little boy, a very happy Christmas, love, Dad.'*

'Look at that Nita,' said Tony with tears in his eyes, 'he's signed himself, 'love, Dad.'

Tony Spencer was a grown man, but he couldn't help it. He read the only letter he'd ever received from his father over and over again and he wept as he read. But he was not unhappy. God had been so good to him. He had his dear wife, his beautiful little son and now he was going to meet his father. He had longed and prayed for this for so many years while he was growing up that he could hardly believe it. What a wonderful New Year 1960 was going to be.

Brothers in uniform

CHAPTER 27

Shattered Dreams

After receiving a letter from his father to say that he would love to meet him, Tony wrote again and explained that he had been given a Barratts shop in Bristol to manage. They had talked on the 'phone. Tony had heard his Father's voice for the very first time.

Just a couple of days before his twenty-sixth birthday, Tony was serving in the shop full of customers when he noticed a gentleman come in who was wearing a dark overcoat and a trilby hat. He went over to him and said:

'Sit over there Dad. I'll be with you in a minute.' He knew without a shadow of a doubt that it was his father. He'd never seen him and had no idea what his father looked like, but when his Father walked into Barratts on that wet and windy February day, he knew. Peter Spencer was taken aback. He had not expected his son to recognise him straight away.

Tony cleared the shop of customers quickly and went over to his Father. 'You are my Dad aren't you?' 'Yes,' said Peter Spencer - 'I'm your Dad!'

Long lost Father and son walked down the high street together to a little restaurant and ordered lunch. Tony was full of questions he was bursting to ask his Father, but the most urgent tumbled out:

'Why Dad, why did you do it? Why did you leave us?'

Just for a second his Father looked nonplussed, confused, totally out of his depth. He hadn't expected to be so forcibly challenged about the past in quite that way.

'It was very difficult Anthony,' he said, not quite knowing where to begin. 'I can't expect you to understand.'

'I've waited twenty-six years to hear your side of the story, Dad!' said Tony anxiously.

'It's very difficult living with someone who drinks, not just socially, but every day and every night. I didn't realise before we were married that your mother had a serious drinking problem. Then the baby came and we had rows and fights.' He sighed, lit a cigarette and offered one to Tony. 'Coming home every night to a mess. Nothing done. The baby always crying. I didn't know what to do. Then another baby was on the way. All she could think about was getting back to work. She hated being in the flat. She said she wasn't cut out to be a housewife and a mother. That was the trouble! I couldn't live my life like that. I had to get away.'

'But what about us, Dad?' said Tony angrily. 'Mum couldn't look after us, so she farmed us out. The Aunts couldn't have us. What were we supposed to do? Nobody wanted us!'

Peter Spencer hadn't really considered the boys. It was between him and Freda. They were too young to know anything about it. He was shocked by the pain and anguish in Anthony's voice.

'But it was better when we went to Canada during the war,' said Tony. 'Aunt Gladys took us. Did you know about that?'

'No,' said his Father flatly. 'After the divorce no-one answered my letters.'

'When we came back from Canada, did Aunt Gladys get in touch with you before we were placed in an orphanage Dad? That was unbelievable for us. You see we knew that we weren't orphans. We had a mother and a father - somewhere!' He couldn't stop the anger and resentment rising up within him. 'I was sure that if Aunt Gladys let you know you would have prevented it. You would have looked after us!'

Peter Spencer frowned and shifted uncomfortably in his seat. 'Evelyn and I would certainly have had one of you to come to live with us,' he said.

Yes, thought Tony, but which one!

'In any case,' continued Peter Spencer, 'I didn't know anything about your being placed in an orphanage!'

'I suppose Aunt Gladys never told you that I joined the navy? Of course, she didn't. I loved it Dad. I became a yeoman signalman. You would have been so proud of me.'

His Father sighed. 'I must say Anthony that things are not at all what I expected them to be. I came to the conclusion a long time ago that you were both better off without me. After all, Godfrey was only a toddler and you weren't even born when I left. I honestly had no idea that things turned out so badly for you boys!'

It was obvious to Tony that he was putting his Father through it, but he couldn't help himself. He had waited so long for this day - it was time.

'I'm only sorry that I didn't make Aunt Gladys give me your address years ago Dad,' said Tony. 'In the end it was because I was worried about Godfrey. You see his marriage is on the rocks. He has a wife and two small boys - the youngest is only a baby. It's as if history is set on repeating itself. I thought you might be able to make him see sense so that he doesn't leave his kids.'

'He's not going to take any notice of me, Anthony,' said his Father. 'I know now that I've let you both down, but I can't undo that. I can't ever make up for the past. I can only be there for you now and in the future if that's what you want. My wife, Evelyn, is a good woman. We have a son, Phillip. She knows all about you and is looking forward to meeting you soon.'

'Can I make arrangements for us to meet up with Godfrey, Dad? He's feeling very rough just now.'

'Yes, of course,' said his Dad. 'I'd love to meet him and his family too.'

Tony left his Father to finish his business visits. He was a Sales Manager and Engineer for a lift company. Then he made his way home to Box.

'How did it go then?' Nita asked him anxiously as soon as he let himself into the flat.

'Very well,' he said. 'No recriminations, but I got everything off my chest. He answered all my questions, but it turns out he didn't have a clue about anything to do with us. The Aunts and my Mother wouldn't let him get anywhere near us. He didn't know we were taken to Canada and he wasn't told that we had to go into an orphanage because there was no-one to look after us when we came back.'

He looked tired and drained. Nita could see that meeting his Father had really affected him. She could only hope that it would all be for the best, in the end.

Tony rang up his brother the very next day and was so excited that he couldn't contain himself.

'Calm down, old mate,' said Godfrey. 'I can't make head nor tail of what you're saying.'

'I've met Dad, Godfrey! He wants to meet you. Could we all meet up somewhere in London and go out for a meal?'

'I'm not sure about that,' said Godfrey doubtfully. 'It's a bit late in the day for meeting up with absent fathers as far as I'm concerned.'

'C'mon Godfrey, give him a chance,' said Tony. 'He's not half as bad as he's been painted all these years.'

The three men did meet up on Waterloo Station. Tony met up with his Father and together they found Godfrey waiting near the main entrance. Tony introduced his Father. It seemed a ridiculous charade to Godfrey.

Tony chattered away nine-to-the-dozen to the both of them like a little boy just out from school. Godfrey was very quiet. When his Father asked him how he was, he answered in monosyllables. When he enquired about his wife and children he stiffened. He reckoned that this stranger was seriously out of order.

Tony filled the strained silences by talking about the wonderful time the boys had had in Canada and how he kept in touch with the Lawrences, their foster parents. That didn't seem to break any ice, so he tried another tack.

'You didn't know that Godfrey has plans to set up his own business, did you Dad? He's the clever one in the family. The one with the brains!'

Godfrey listened sullenly to his brother rabitting on and wished to God he would stop.

'I'll have to be going soon,' he said to his brother. He couldn't be persuaded to stay even to drink his coffee. Tony followed him outside the café. 'It's no good Anthony,' he said. 'It was all a mistake. I should never have come.'

'Perhaps some other time, Godfrey?' said Tony clutching at straws.

'No, I'm not interested. I don't want any further contact and that's final. I'll get in touch with you and Nita in a week or two.'

Then without a backward glance at his Father, he was gone.

Tony returned to his Father full of excuses for his brother's abrupt exit. 'He's just a bit under the weather. He's got a lot on his mind. Told me to say 'goodbye and all that!'

But Peter Spencer wasn't fooled for a moment. 'I made a hash of it, didn't I?' he said. 'He made it very obvious that he doesn't want to know me and I can't say that I blame him.'

'That may be how he's feeling at the moment,' said Tony not willing to admit defeat in realising his long held dream of becoming a family. 'He'll come around, one day.'

'I meant what I said the other day,' said his Father. 'I'd like to be there for you and your little family if you'll have me, Anthony. I'm sure that we can work something out?'

'Yes, you're right,' said Tony wistfully. 'We can still work something out.'

Nita & Tony's Dad

CHAPTER 28

Not the End...

There was no time for Tony to be distraught over his brother's domestic and financial troubles. His dear wife, Nita was nearing her time. They embarked for Gloucester and the loving ministrations of Dolly Barton were on hand when Nita went into labour for the second time. There was great relief and joy in the Barton household when a little girl, Shirley Louise Spencer was handed to her proud father, on May 18th 1960 – apple blossom time! And what did little Phillip Spencer make of his new baby sister? Not much, by all accounts.

Peter Spencer did not forget his promise to his son. After being informed of the safe arrival of a little daughter, he sent Anthony and Nita an invitation.

'Evelyn and I were delighted to learn of your little daughter's safe arrival in May. Now that we are well into the summer, we would like to invite you to come and stay with us. Evelyn loves babies and we've got lots of fun things to occupy young Phillip. So how about it?'

Once again Nita was hesitant. 'It'll be a lot of bother for Evelyn, Tony,' she said. 'There's the nappies and things and the baby's not sleeping through the night yet. Our Phillip gets into everything, you know he does. We'll be disturbing them!'

Tony always enjoyed taking the bull by the horns and firmly vanquishing the jitters wherever they reared their heads and did so in this case.

'Well, Dad and his wife have given us a firm date and it's for a week. They must have thought about it and made up their minds that this is the right time. We're going Nita, and that's all there is to be said about it!'

They would have to take public transport of course. Not many ordinary young people like themselves had a family car in those days, but they had recently moved into their very own house in Oldland Common, near Bristol. They had taken out a mortgage for the princely sum of £1,950 for a three-bedroomed semi, no garage, after persuading the National Provincial Bank to loan them the essential down payment of £65. True, it didn't have much in it and it was going to take a lot of scrimping and saving to repay the mortgage, but Nita was always good at that.

Tony was confident, one might even say jubilant when the day finally arrived and they found themselves walking up the pathway to 375 Baker Street, Enfield. However, it must be said that Nita, clutching their young son's little hand while Tony proudly pushed the pram, was not feeling quite so confident and jubilant.

Tony rang the bell. The door opened and out bounded an enormous lumbering black poodle. Nita stiffled a scream - after all it was only a dog, but Tony was all smiles. In the meantime, Evelyn Spencer, the lady of the house said the usual thing that one says to strangers at such a time as this:

'Oh, don't mind Rastus. He's as soft as a kitten. He wouldn't hurt a fly!'

Whereupon Rastus knocked two and half year Phillip down to the ground and stood guard over him. Phillip started bawling and Nita was not at all convinced that they had done the right thing in coming.

'Welcome,' said Evelyn. 'I've heard so much about you from Peter. It's good to meet you at last. Come in, come in.'

She was a small dark-haired little lady, perfectly composed, smartly dressed, nothing out of place from head to toe, but Tony noticed straight away that her eyes were smiling and her greeting was genuine.

Peter Spencer came down the stairs and made straight for little Phillip who was still recovering from his recent encounter with a big sloppy dog. 'Come on little chap,' he said. 'Let's you and I and Daddy and Rastus go out and play in the garden while the ladies get to know each other.'

'You see,' said Tony to his wife. 'I told you everything was going to be all right!'

It took a little longer for Nita to be reassured. 'I ought to go and look after Phillip,' she said to Evelyn. 'He doesn't know his way around and he might be a bit of a nuisance.'

'Of course he won't,' said Evelyn laughing. 'Peter knows exactly what to do with little boys. We had one of our own once,' she added wistfully pointing to a silver-framed photograph of her own Phillip when he was a little boy of 6 or 7. 'I'm afraid you won't be meeting him this time. He's away walking in the Peak district with some friends, but there will be other times, I'm sure.'

Baby Shirley started to grizzle. Nita picked up her precious little bundle and whispered comforting words to her as she held her close. 'What a beautiful baby,' said Evelyn. 'I should have loved a little daughter, but it wasn't meant to be. Never mind. We can all enjoy bringing up little Shirley, can't we!'

That won Nita over!

In the balmy days and nights that followed, Peter Tony and young Phillip got on like a house on fire and Nita and Evelyn, happily shared the chores and the cooking and even the nappy-changing.

Nita learned that because Evelyn's father had been with the British army in India, she had grown up in in a house full of servants. It was obvious in the way she ran her household, effortlessly, like everything else she did and the result was a peaceful happy domain. In fact, Nita was amazed that she was able to adapt so well to the disruption that she and her young family had brought to her routine.

They didn't have to stay in the house. Peter Spencer was the proud owner of an Austin A55 car and he took great pleasure in taking Tony and the family out and about to explore the surrounding countryside and beyond. They took picnics, a ball and a kite and there was never a dull moment with Rastus chasing the ball, the kite and even some wily jack-rabbits.

One evening when Peter and Tony were enjoying a quiet smoke after dinner, they wandered down to the bottom of the garden and Peter showed Tony an old Morgan engine. 'You see this old engine,' said Peter. My son, Phillip and I have been working on it for years, hoping to get it up and running one of these days and into that MG body over there. I don't know if we'll ever get it on the road, but it's been a lot of fun working on it together.' He sighed. 'It's amazing where the time goes, Anthony. One minute they're little nippers, like your young son and the next their eighteen, young men. Then they're off and we've lost them!'

All too soon it was Friday night. They were due to go home the next day. It had been a terrific week. They had been made so welcome, everything had gone so well and yet... there was something wrong. Nita noticed that Tony's sunny mood had changed.

'Well dear,' she ventured, 'has something happened to upset you, or are you just sad that we have to go back home tomorrow and leave all of this?'

Tony looked slowly around the bedroom. It belonged to his half-brother, Phillip. It was a large room with a big window overlooking the back garden; simply decorated, plain but tasteful. There were pictures of Phillip and his pals on the tall chest of drawers and others of him when he was a little boy taken with his Mum and Dad and lots of books on engineering and maths, that sort of thing.

'I don't know,' said Tony sadly. I'm beginning to …realise what Godfrey and I missed as boys. Look at their son. He was brought up in this house from the day he was born: wanted, loved and everything else. My father didn't even know what I was when I was born. No-one bothered to tell him. And quite honestly Nita, I marvel at their relationship, Dad and Evelyn's. It's just wonderful to watch them together. They're like a couple of lovebirds and they've been together for well over twenty years. It's so much better for the kids if the parents love each other, isn't it?'

Nita was distraught. 'But Tony, we have that don't we?' she said, worried about the effect this new relationship with his father was having on her husband.

'Yes, of course we do,' said Tony giving his wife a big hug. 'Of course, we do.'

But the next day as they were busy packing things up and getting ready for Peter to drive them to the station, it was obvious to Nita that Tony felt no better and even his father noticed a subtle change in the attitude of his newly found son.

'Anything the matter Anthony?' he enquired as they took their last turn around the garden, not really expecting anything earth-shattering to be forthcoming.

'Yes, there is,' said Tony seriously. 'Godfrey and I have missed so much Dad like that old Morgan engine stuck down the bottom of the garden that you and your Phillip have been working on for years. And we never had a Dad to take us fishing. Things like that Dad. We were cast-offs, unwanted; pushed from pillar to post and then dumped in an orphanage. Well you don't get over it that easily.

And when you get older, you are soon made to realise that you haven't got the education that others have had. Simply due to the mistake that others made before you were even born. Even the Aunts didn't know what to do with a couple of their sister's unwanted boys! I don't think Godfrey and I will ever get over it, not really.

I had thought that once I got to know you - my own Dad, things would be all right. Everything would fall into place, but now, I'm not so sure.'

Peter Spencer was stunned. Little Phillip came running up to them and pulled at his grandpa's trousers. 'Come on grandpa,' he cried, 'Come and play, come and play!'

All too soon it was time to hug and thank their hostess for giving them a very happy week and to receive her assurances that there would be many more get-togethers in the future and then they were bundled into the car and were waving 'goodbye'.

Nita had no idea what had passed between Tony and his father while they were out in the back garden chatting before getting their cases put into the boot.

Just before their train came into the station, Nita turned to Peter. 'Well, we've had a really lovely week with you and Evelyn, haven't we Tony.' she said. And even though her shyness threatened to get the better of her, she leaned forward and gave him a big hug and a kiss. 'Thank you so much for having us!' she whispered.

'Thank you for coming,' said Peter. 'I haven't seen Evelyn so happy for a long time. She always wanted a big family you know and you've brought us both a new lease of life.'

Then he turned towards his son - 'I do hope you'll come and see us again. You see, I don't want to lose you Anthony, now that I've found you!'

Spencer - young family - 1961

216

Lightning Source UK Ltd.
Milton Keynes UK
29 September 2009

144304UK00002B/29/P